AND
BABY
MAKES
THREE

ALSO BY JOHN AND JULIE GOTTMAN

Ten Lessons to Transform Your Marriage
with Joan DeClaire

ALSO BY JOHN GOTTMAN

Meta-Emotion: How Families Communicate Emotionally
with Lynn Katz and Carole Hooven

The Heart of Parenting: How to Raise
an Emotionally Intelligent Child
with Joan DeClaire

The Analysis of Change

Why Marriages Succeed or Fail
with Nan Silver

What Predicts Divorce?

The Seven Principles for Making Marriage Work
with Nan Silver

The Relationship Cure
with Joan DeClaire

The Marriage Clinic

ALSO BY JULIE GOTTMAN

The Marriage Clinic Casebook

JOHN GOTTMAN, PH.D. and
JULIE SCHWARTZ GOTTMAN, PH.D.

 CROWN PUBLISHERS • NEW YORK

AND
BABY
MAKES
THREE

The Six-Step Plan for

Preserving Marital Intimacy and Rekindling Romance

After Baby Arrives

Published in the United States by Crown Publishers, an imprint of the Crown
Publishing Group, a division of Random House, Inc., New York.
www.crownpublishing.com

Crown is a trademark and the Crown colophon is a registered trademark of
Random House, Inc.

Library of Congress Cataloging-in-Publication Data
Gottman, John Mordechai.
   And baby makes three: the six-step plan for preserving marital intimacy and
   rekindling romance after baby arrives / John Gottman, and Julie Schwartz
   Gottman—1st ed.
   1. Parents—Psychology. 2. Married people—Psychology. 3. Sex in marriage.
   I. Gottman, Julie Schwartz. II. Title.
HQ755.8.G69   2007
646.7'8—dc22   2006025625
ISBN 978-1-4000-9737-1

Printed in the United States of America

DESIGN BY ELINA D. NUDELMAN

10 9 8 7 6 5 4 3 2 1

First Edition

We dedicate this book
to our beloved daughter, Moriah Sara,
who gave us profound joy
in our becoming three

CONTENTS

CONTENTS

AND
BABY
MAKES
THREE

INTRODUCTION

We loved being pregnant. Parenting had been hard to come by for us. Four years of grueling fertility procedures meant Julie was nearly forty, and John forty-eight, when pregnancy finally and miraculously arrived. In September, with Julie in her seventh month, we took a break from work and drove from Seattle to Yellowstone Park. In the car with windows open and hair flying, we sang along with Bonnie Raitt's tape *Nick of Time* at the top of our lungs. Cruising through Idaho, we had some of those great close conversations that you remember for years. Finally arriving late the next night, we rented a simple rustic cabin and collapsed into deep sleep. But at 3 a.m. we both woke up. As we turned toward each other, John whispered, "It just came to me. I know what the baby's name should be." Julie asked, "What?" John replied, "Moriah." Julie's jaw dropped and she exclaimed, "That's the name I was just dreaming about!" We curled up again and dozed. It was just us and little Moriah, waiting to be born.

A few months later, in mid-December, the day was warm and beautiful like spring. Julie was very pregnant and huge. We got up, made toast and eggs, and she smiled and said, "I have to buy a winter coat." Shaking his head, John looked at her like she was nuts and said, "Wait until after the baby is born." "No," she said. John calmly repeated himself, thinking she hadn't understood, "Just wait, because if it fits you now, it won't ever fit you again. You're big, dear." And she said, "No, I want to buy a winter coat right now." So John thought of his motto—never argue with a pregnant woman. Sighing, he said, "OK. Let's go get the coat." Off we went. Julie bought a winter coat three sizes bigger than her usual. Content, she put it on.

Then, as we exited the store, Julie said, "I want us to get chains for the car." Exasperated, John said, "Look, that makes absolutely no sense. Look around you—it's a beautiful warm winter day. And it never really snows in Seattle." Julie said, "I don't care. I want chains for the car."

From the clothing store, we drove to a car-supply shop. The man behind the counter was big and burly. He said, "Yeah, I got chains for your car, but look, man, it never even snows here, so don't waste your money. You don't need 'em." John just pointed at Julie standing in the store, with her big belly and wearing her huge winter coat. The guy behind the counter nodded, winked at John, and said, "Oh, yeah, I get it." He retreated to the back of the shop to get the chains.

As we left, Julie said, "We have to get the chains put on the car." John said, "Well, I can't put them on, but our mechanic probably can." By this time he knew better than to argue. At the garage, the guy said, "Are you nuts? It's a beautiful day, a few clouds maybe, but it's nothing. Anyway, I am very busy right now." John just pointed at Julie standing in the garage. The mechanic nodded. "Oh, yeah, I get it. Look, get yourself some lunch at the Greek place next door, and the car will be ready when you're done eating." We ate, and an hour later drove home with the car bouncing and bumping on the bare streets.

Around 5 p.m., the usual mild December breeze became freakishly still. It grew very dark. A chill swept through the house. Then a few snowflakes, ornate and beautiful, floated down. Suddenly, the temperature dropped, and continued dropping. The wind gathered speed. In an hour, the house was like a freezer. As we looked out the window, we saw the snow flying by and trees bent double by the wind. An enormous blizzard raged outside. John hadn't seen one like this since leaving Illinois five years earlier. Later, the headlines would call it the century storm, the largest snowstorm to hit Seattle in a hundred years. It snowed two feet in four hours. Drifts piled up to five feet. In the mountains, the wind was clocked at ninety-eight miles an hour.

That evening, as Julie climbed the stairs, water poured down her legs. She cried, "John, it's time!" Then, a little grim but smug, she pulled on her winter coat. We piled into the car toting our overnight bag. With perfectly fitting chains on our tires, we sailed up steep Capitol Hill to our hospital high at the top. Along the way, abandoned cars lay askew in the road. The entire city was stranded. There were lines six hours long to buy chains, and the snow kept coming down. The temperature read near zero.

At the hospital, our obstetrician smiled at us. It was several hours beyond her normal shift, but she couldn't drive home in the snow, so weren't we in luck? Nurses couldn't leave, either, and the next shift couldn't come in. There we were, one little happy group.

A few hours later, the contractions came every five minutes. Julie's face was contorted with pain, but it still wasn't delivery time. We walked around the hospital. "Squat, do the quick breath, and walk." John coached Julie like he'd learned in birth preparation classes. Despite the hours of labor pain, delivery wasn't even close. We retired to our room, where John slept on a chair next to Julie's bed. Twenty hours passed. Nurses who were stuck at the hospital now slept in all the hospital's extra beds. Julie lay still, contracting and waiting. She held on to John's hand.

Late the next day, finally, it was delivery time. Julie was raced into the birthing room with John beside her. As Julie was set up for delivery, John and her attending anesthesiologist talked about electrocardiograms. John asked questions, and the doctor drew diagrams on Julie's pillow as he explained the monitoring equipment to John. Suddenly, Julie yelled, "Hey, you guys!"

As John incredulously watched and held one of Julie's legs, Moriah's dark crown appeared. Then her face. With her big gorgeous eyes, Moriah looked around very calmly. Then she saw John. Her face seemed to say, "This is very interesting. Who are you?" John thought to himself, "I love that face. I could look at it all day every day for the rest of my life." He was in love. Moriah gave a little whimper. She was handed to Julie, who embraced her, and the baby started to suck. We both cried and cried.

When we brought Moriah home a day later over the icy streets, we were exhausted and happy, and deeply in love with each other and with our baby. In that instant of childbirth, we had intensely connected with all of humanity. We never realized how much we could love. No question—we'd block a Mack truck and give our lives for this baby. Our new vulnerability was overwhelming. If anything happened to her, we'd be finished.

As Moriah slept in the bassinet next to us, we looked at each other and Julie said, "OK, what do we do now?" John said, "Well, they gave us a videotape at the hospital. Let's put it on." We watched as the tape told us about all the services Swedish Medical Center offered. Treatments for cancer and broken bones, first-aid tips, you name it—everything but babies. We were disappointed, a little bewildered, and exhausted. Just as we lay down, the baby began to stir. Instinctively, we put her between us. Smiling, we began to softly sing, "Just Molly and me, and baby makes three." We both fell asleep with little Moriah between us. We were a family.

THE RESEARCH

"What do we do now?" Don't most of us ask this question after our first baby's arrival? This is the topic that became John's driving curiosity from that night forward. But it took eight years before he could finally begin to answer it.

By the time Moriah was around eight years old, John was known in Seattle as an expert on couples' relationships. One day early in 1998, a special call came in. It was a woman who represented both Children's Hospital and a newspaper called *Seattle's Child*. The woman asked John if he would give a public talk on how a first baby affects a couple's relationship. John thought about it; he did have some data from a long-term study he was doing on newly-weds, and by that time about fifty of these couples had already had babies. He figured that if he carefully reviewed this data, he could present some interesting findings.

The data shocked us. Sixty-seven percent of these couples had become very unhappy with each other during the first three years of their baby's life. Only 33 percent of these couples remained content with each other. Even though this minority faced the same stresses after their baby's birth as the other 67 percent, they coped much better with the strain. Of course, they encountered bumps along the way, too, but they enjoyed a much smoother journey overall.

We called these couples the "masters" of the transition to parenthood. Clearly, all couples who were becoming parents faced struggles in their relationships. Crying babies weren't easy on romance. But the masters found a way to successfully navigate the shoals that had shipwrecked the other couples, the "disasters" of this transition. So we asked, how were the couples who were masters different from those who were disasters? Were they different even days after the wedding, well before they even had their first child?

For inspiration, we looked at the pioneering research done by our friends Carolyn and Philip Cowan at the University of California, Berkeley. In their study, they ran support groups for couples that lasted six months, beginning in the last trimester of pregnancy. They compared these couples with a different set of couples in a control group who had no such group experience. Couples were selected at random to be in the support groups or in the control group.

The Cowans found that the couples who experienced the support groups changed in many ways. Perhaps most important, the couples realized that the stresses they encountered were not the result of relationships gone sour. Most of their fellow couples in the groups were colliding with problems just like the ones they were having.

The Cowans' research was a revelation; it showed that we are all in the same soup when our babies arrive. Like the Cowans' couples, the moms and dads in our study were confronting similar difficulties. The difference was that the masters in our study coped far better with these problems than our disasters. Sadly, the couples that were disasters were twice as likely to end up in divorce court.

For John to prepare for his talk at Children's Hospital, he and his student, Alyson Shapiro, extensively analyzed the masters and disasters in our study. How did these two sets of couples handle conflict differently? What did they do to remain emotionally connected? How did they try to live their dreams? It turned out that there were tremendous differences between them. The news of how these masters and disasters differed became the subject for John's talk at Children's Hospital.

To our amazement, it was standing room only that night! Everyone seemed deeply concerned about preserving their relationships after their babies arrived. Many of the moms were still pregnant. Some parents had tiny new babies in their arms. Others had older kids along, too. And there were lots of dads present, not just moms. Fifty people had to be turned away at the door because with seats and standing room filled, no more space was left in the lecture hall. Nobody expected this many people.

Another talk was scheduled, and then another. The talks were advertised as "Bringing Baby Home: Preserving Intimacy After Baby." During these evenings, you could hear a pin drop. These couples desperately wanted to know what to do, how to stay close, how to be good parents. There were many, many questions.

After one talk, some of the couples asked John, "Is this all you have to offer?" And he had to reply, "I'm sorry, but it is." They politely informed him, "Well, it's a good start, but it isn't enough."

John agreed with them. He went home, beckoned Julie to sit down, and we began an extensive conversation.

What could we offer that could help these parents? Julie had treated over eight hundred patients in thirty-plus years of clinical work, many of whom were parents. Their suffering had arisen from depression, post-traumatic stress disorder, sexual- and physical-abuse histories, and the garden-variety stresses of life. For many, their concerns for their kids were why they sought treatment in the first place.

Meanwhile, John had conducted twenty-five studies of couples in over thirty years as a professor and researcher. In the last thirteen years, 222 out of 302 couples had had babies, and the babies were studied, too.

In addition, we had cofounded the Gottman Institute in 1996. Combining research and clinical experience, we had created a couples' weekend workshop for the institute and had offered it since '96 to sellout crowds. (It's still offered today.)

We taught the workshop together, using role plays, examples from our own marriage, research information, and nuts-and-bolts exercises that couples practiced. The workshop focused on deepening friendship, managing conflict, and sharing values to heal distressed relationships and enhance healthy ones. Eighty-five percent of the couples taking it reported making a major breakthrough on a gridlocked conflict during it. We must have been doing something right.

Bringing our combined years of experience to the table, we now set to work. In two months, we designed a workshop for couples having a baby called "Bringing Baby Home." It combined the principles from our couples' workshop with additional ones tailored for new parents. Then, at the same hospital where our daughter had been born ten years earlier, we conducted a research study to evaluate the workshop's effectiveness. The results were very encouraging, and we began another, longer-term study that has now been completed.

It has now been eight years since that first talk—a great journey together, for our couples and ourselves.

This book is the result of that journey.

What have we learned from the research? First, let us tell you the facts of what happened to the majority of couples, the disasters in our study, before we designed our workshop.

WHAT HAPPENS TO A COUPLE
WHEN A BABY ARRIVES? THE BARE FACTS

We know that approximately 3.6 million babies are born to couples every year in the United States of America. This should be a time of great joy, right? Unfortunately, research from many laboratories, including our own, has shown that for many couples these joys are fleeting moments at best.

Our research study found that after the first baby was born, relationship satisfaction dropped significantly for two-thirds of the couples. Conflict within the relationship and hostility toward each other dramatically increased. They found themselves fighting much more. Their emotional intimacy deteriorated. They became bewildered and exhausted. Not surprisingly, their passion, sex, and romance plummeted.

Like many other researchers who had studied new mothers, we also found that postpartum depression in our mothers (and some fathers) occurred more commonly than we anticipated. After a baby's arrival, parents often became fatigued, sleepless, and irritable. In many cases, exhaustion deepened into depression. In addition, parents who were disasters failed to realize the mountain of work they'd face once their baby arrived. Afterward, they battled repeatedly in the house about who should do what. Finally, both parents ended up feeling unappreciated, neglected, and lonely.

Over the course of the next months, as Baby took center stage, the romance between these parents dissolved. Some of them became so isolated that an affair ruptured their connection altogether. Others slowly slid down a cascade toward miserable coexistence and eventual separation. Sadly, it was the majority of our parents who made this descent after the birth of their first baby.

What happened to the babies in the meantime? There was a severe strain on their intellectual and emotional development that put the babies' normal development in jeopardy.

Babies need parents who respond when they have a need, who soothe them when they're upset, calm them when they're frightened, and play enthusiastically with them when they're ready for fun. But when parents are distressed and lonely or depressed, they are less responsive to their babies. Babies' crying only irritates them, babies' fears annoy them, and babies' playfulness feels too demanding. This is especially true when parents are at war with each other.

Babies are also amazingly attuned to orient and respond to their parents' faces and voices. But when babies cry with fear at the hostility they hear in those voices, their cries become a distraction from the parental business at hand—fighting. Distressed parents often want their babies to be quiet and not need them so much, like dolls in a crib. This creates a withdrawn parent-child emotional relationship. Unhappily married parents may also be intrusive to force their babies into preferable behavior—like shutting up.

In our study, babies raised by unhappy parents suffered developmentally. They lagged behind the babies of contented parents both intellectually and emotionally. Speech occurred later, potty training was delayed, and the ability to self-soothe was slow in coming. Studies by psychologist Tiffany Field with depressed parents suggest that some of these delays would last. The children would probably be lagging behind for years to come.

From this research, the message is clear: The greatest gift a couple can give their baby is a loving relationship, because that relationship nourishes Baby's development. The stronger the connection between parents, the healthier the child can grow, both emotionally and intellectually. Children can't thrive in stormy seas. No family wants to end up in the disaster column. The good news is that when we looked at our master couples, it was clear that no family has to! The methods our masters practiced are steps that any of us can use to keep our families strong and healthy. When followed, these steps proved in our studies to predict a positive outcome for families.

Giving you the ingredients to help you to create and preserve your loving family is the goal of this book.

HOW TO HAVE A STRONG AND LOVING RELATIONSHIP: OUR RECIPE

This book will provide you with a six-step recipe for creating and maintaining your healthy family. Here's what you'll learn to do.

1. *Realize that we're all in the same soup.*
2. *Delight in responding to your baby.*
3. *Cool down your conflicts.*
4. *Savor each other by building a strong friendship and a zesty sex life.*
5. *Add warm fathering to the mix.*
6. *Create an enriching legacy.*

The chapters in this book are our instructions for this recipe, step by step. They come from our workshop on the transition to parenthood and the research we conducted to evaluate it.

What can you expect if you follow these steps? Our research findings, summarized below, suggest:

• YOU CAN PREVENT RELATIONSHIP MELTDOWN. For the couples in our study that didn't receive the workshop (the control group), relationship quality between parents deteriorated significantly and steadily over a three-year period. For couples who received the workshop and learned the skills of the masters (the workshop group), relationship quality remained high.

• YOU CAN PREVENT ESCALATING HOSTILITY. For parents in the control group, hostility increased dramatically during the baby's first year of life, but for couples in the workshop group, hostility remained minimal.

• YOU CAN PREVENT POSTPARTUM DEPRESSION. Sixty-six and one-half percent of mothers in the control group developed symptoms of post-partum depression, in contrast to only 22.5 percent of mothers in the workshop group. This represents a tremendous difference in the oc-currence of postpartum depression.

• YOU CAN POSITIVELY INFLUENCE YOUR BABY'S DEVELOPMENT. When the babies in our study were three months old, we scored videotapes of moms and dads playing together with their baby. Here's what we found: Dads who took the workshop were both more cooperative and less competitive with their partners than dads in the control group. Also, fathers who took the workshop were significantly more positive and had a lot more fun with their babies than fathers in the control group. Moreover, the babies whose parents attended the workshop were significantly more tuned in to their dads and their moms than babies whose parents were in the control group. These babies from the workshop group also had many more intense positive emotions and fewer intense negative emotions than babies from the control group. The babies of parents in the workshop also learned language sooner than the babies of parents in the control group. From these findings, we concluded that the babies whose parents took the work-shop were now on the right course of emotional development.

And if you follow these steps, we think you'll be on the right course, too, both for yourselves and for your baby.

On that frigid night when our daughter was born, our lives dra-matically changed. Like many parents, now we needed to balance career time with infant care. There were the inevitable sleep problems, nanny failures, and day-care tribulations. Plus, our daughter suffered multiple ear infections that landed us in the ER, always at 3 a.m., it seemed. On one of these visits, we had to shield her from a raging couple duking it out in the waiting room. And as part of the "sandwich" generation, between our daughter and John's beloved, diabetic mother, we traveled frequently enough through those hospital doors to carve out our own personal pathway. Combined with weaving our work worlds together, there was plenty of stress to go around. Through it all though, we garnered the valuable lessons taught us by our couples in lab and clinical office. We practiced them, learned, and loved. And grew closer still.

We experienced exquisite moments of joy holding our daughter together between us. Fifteen years later, we still do. And so can you.

1

REALIZE WE'RE ALL IN THE SAME SOUP

Jim wakes up early one morning in an amorous mood. He reaches over and touches his wife's breast. She sits bolt upright and exclaims, "Those are for the baby!" Jim is crushed. He dashes out of bed and jumps in the shower.

Margarita and Carlos are about to make love one night when the baby starts crying. Carlos jokes, "Damn! This baby must have a radar for our lovemaking. He's saying, 'No sibs for me!'" Margarita doesn't laugh. She gets up. Carlos grabs her nightgown, pulls her back, and, a little irritably says, "Stay. He can just calm himself. The trouble is you never give him the chance to." Margarita frowns, once again gets up, and Carlos utters another "Damn!" under his breath. She hears him. When she returns to bed a while later, she expects Carlos to be angry. But surprisingly, Carlos apologizes and says that he understands why she had to go to the baby. He offers to go the next time the baby cries. Now *she* cries, but in gratitude. Exhausted, both of them feel closer again and cuddle together. They fall asleep in each other's arms, as the baby sleeps through his first night.

Across the street, Debbie comes to breakfast with her baby. Her husband, Harry, sits down to eat, too, but pulls his chair over to the portable TV. Debbie says, "Can't you turn that thing off and spend breakfast with me and the baby?" Harry says, "Shut up and stop nagging! I just want to hear the news before work. Anyway, what do you want me for? You sure as hell don't want me at night. I'm pretty worthless to you, aren't I? What do you care how hard I work, or when I help out around here? You're the one driving me away. All you want is to be with that baby." Debbie yells, "What is it with you men? Can't you get it that when a woman has a baby hanging on her all day, she doesn't want a man hanging on her all night?" Harry gets up and leaves with the portable TV, slamming the door behind him.

A few blocks away, there's a different picture. Jason and his partner, Shanique, play with their six-month-old son, Marcus, who's getting a fresh diaper on the changing table. Marcus is watching his parents with eyes like saucers. Jason sings, "I'm gonna . . . get . . . your . . . belly!" and he gives Marcus a big loud kiss on the belly. Marcus giggles and flashes Jason a gorgeous smile. Jason and Shanique both dive in, tickling and blowing on their baby's tummy. The baby wiggles and squeals with laughter. Shanique and Jason pick him up, fresh and clean, and dance over the living-room floor.

What's the difference between these families? They all have new babies, they all face the same joys and the same stresses, and yet some are so happy, and some are not. In our research, we've discovered that everyone has the best of intentions after their babies are born. But some couples weather the transition beautifully, others stumble but regain their footing, while still others fall . . . and keep falling.

First, though, before we examine what distinguishes one group of couples from another, let's answer a more fundamental question: Who *is* having babies in this country?

BABIES ARE MOSTLY BORN TO COUPLES

About 4.5 million babies are born each year in the United States. The vast majority are born to married couples, not single moms. But the numbers are changing dramatically. In 1980, the estimate was that 18.4 percent of all babies were born to single moms. By 2003, the figure increased to 34.6 percent—over a third of all babies born in this country. These figures suggest that single motherhood is on the rise. There's a fear that children born to single moms are at greater risk for poverty, neglect, and maltreatment. Some say that if these babies were born to couples committed to staying together, their families would be much better off.

These statistics are highly misleading. A recent study in twenty-one American cities found that unwed mothers are rarely alone. Independent of race and ethnicity, a whopping 82 percent of these moms are romantically involved with the fathers of their babies. Sixty percent of these couples live together and are gallantly struggling to make it. So the overwhelming majority of unwed mothers are partnered already with the dads of their babies. "Single" motherhood, at least in the first year of Baby's life, is largely a myth.

As we travel around the nation conducting our workshops for birth educators, we also see men in every social class and ethnic group wanting to be better fathers and partners. Many men have experienced absentee fathers whom they either have never met or who disappeared early from their families. They don't want to repeat their fathers' mistakes. They want a different life for themselves. Many of them want families even more than friends or careers.

All told, this means that nearly all babies are born to couples, married or not. And couples are showing a profound commitment these days to creating not just babies, but healthy families. That's what this book is all about.

THE SOUP WE'RE ALL IN

There's an old joke about a man who goes to a restaurant, and after his soup arrives he calls the waiter over. He says to the waiter, "Taste the soup." The waiter assures him that this soup has taken weeks to prepare, and that the chef is one of the finest in the city.

The man again says to the waiter, "Taste the soup." The waiter offers more assurances. He brings over framed restaurant reviews that all mention the soup. The man nods and smiles and again says to the waiter, "Taste the soup." Finally, exasperated, the waiter says, "All right. I'll taste the soup . . . Where's the spoon?" "Aha!" the man says.

There's no way for us to know how our lives will change after our baby arrives. We think we'll be full of joy. Everyone tells us that there's nothing more exciting than a new baby. Babies are the natural culmination of the love we share. They are the dawning of new hope. Babies delight us with their cuteness and draw us into their peaceful, loving world. They are soft and tender, helpless and small. They need us. They call us to love and nurture them. They are also very nice people. They openly greet us, and they eagerly play with us. They engage us, imitate us, and smile at us. Once we get to know our babies, we think, maybe our species is good and fine after all.

But sometimes we find that we may have cooked up a tasty fantasy. Once the realities of new parenthood set in, the stresses stand out, too, like too much salt in a dish.

Our thirteen-year research study with 130 young families uncovered a startling fact: In the first three years after babies were born, a whopping two-thirds of parents experienced a significant drop in their couple relationship quality. Being with Baby tasted so sweet, but being together as partners turned bitter; increases in conflict and hostility soured family life.

If these research results are representative, we're talking about an overwhelming majority of American families who suffer from relationship distress after children come. We heard many stories like these (the following names and identifying details were changed).

Angelica complained that her husband expects her to do almost all of the housework and child care even though she now works half-time. Robert said that he now works not only *full*-time but does a lot of *over*time as well, and that should count for something.

She sarcastically said, "Thank you, Your Highness. But you can change this diaper right now as part of your overtime at home."

He snickered. "No way. I'll change a wet diaper, but the poop ones are all yours."

She did not laugh. She changed the diaper.

Jonathan and Jenny sat on a couch together during an interview. He said, "Jenny's too involved with the baby. She's got no limits. She doesn't get that we have to save our money now. She'll spend a week's salary just so the baby will look cute when she brings him out to her friends. It's like our baby is Barbie. She's totally impractical."

She said, "You don't understand! Our baby outgrows everything so fast. Besides, I am not impractical. I resent that! You're just a cheapskate who doesn't earn enough money. I had to get that new stroller. The old one wasn't safe."

He shot back, "All I ever hear out of your mouth are zingers, nothing but criticism. What about all the good stuff I do?"

She whipped out, "Whenever you do anything, you don't do it right, so I have to do it all over again." She laughed.

He said, "Another zinger."

The two of them ended up sitting next to each other, not talking, stone-faced and looking straight ahead.

These examples are typical. In our research, we score videotapes of couples discussing problems in detail, second by second. Here's what we see: The couples in trouble are critical, defensive, and disrespectful with each other. They are blind to their partner's point of view, and they can't compromise. They often say things they later regret. Not surprisingly, most of these couples have elevated heart rates during their arguments. Their fights feel like tripping through mine fields. Their partners seem like enemies, not allies. Apparently, their partners don't even like them, let alone respect them. Over time, both partners are haunted by feeling unappreciated, neglected, and lonely.

How does this calamity happen when there should only be joy?

The story seems to be this: When a baby arrives, a couple's intimacy deteriorates. Sex, romance, and passion often decline. The relationship shifts its center to the baby. Husbands and wives who were once friends and lovers no longer have time for each other. Dating stops entirely, and long conversations disappear. Both parents get lonely, and can be drawn to others outside the marriage. Most affairs occur after children come. Family time is now battle time.

Worse yet, battles get physical. One U.S. study found that 37 percent of obstetric patients experience domestic violence with their partners. Another study found that 30 percent of domestic violence begins in pregnancy. Is it any wonder that our divorce rate has climbed to 50 percent, and that many of these divorces occur within a few years of babies' births?

Part of the problem is that we think becoming parents shouldn't be a big deal. It seems unthinkable that our new baby could be clutching in his little hands some major stresses. After all, isn't having a baby a happy event? We receive those Hallmark cards that say, "Congratulations!" to celebrate the occasion. And of course, our baby's birth *is* a wonderful occasion. But maybe, in tiny black letters, the cards should also read, "Say good-bye to your romance."

Does it have to be this way? Not if we have the skills to create savory family time, instead of sour and bitter moments. The findings of many research studies can help us.

PARENTS ARE VERY STRESSED

As early as 1957, a landmark study by E. E. LeMasters claimed that an astounding 83 percent of new parents went through moderate to severe crisis in the transition to parenthood. Unfortunately, no one believed LeMasters. His claims were initially dismissed—or, at best, strongly debated—because no one could believe such high-percentage numbers could be real. But later, in the 1980s, other studies began to appear, and they confirmed LeMasters's findings. Now, after more than sixteen long-term studies, we know that he was right.

BOTH PARENTS ARE IRRITABLE, OVERLY EMOTIONAL, AND THEY FIGHT A LOT

There is so much to do when a new baby arrives. Babies need to be fed every two hours, including at night. So most babies don't sleep through the night, at least for a while. Also, babies signal their needs by crying. This means that babies cry a lot. Babies cry when they are wet, when they are in pain, when they have gas, when they are scared, when they are lonely, when they need to be held, and when they are hungry.

We parents spend many nights at 3 a.m. walking around the house with our babies trying to help them go to sleep. We dance with our babies, sing to our babies, count to a hundred with our babies, reason with our babies, rock our babies, and bathe our babies. We wipe up baby drool, baby pee, baby poop, and baby spit. We look in mirrors with our babies, go for drives with our babies, play the saxophone to our babies, and take our babies into our parental beds. We sleep with our babies next to us, and we sleep with our babies on top of us. Then we change our babies, feed our babies, take our babies to the park and to the pediatrician. And we buy things for our babies—cribs, playpens, rattles, toys, mobiles, baby music, car seats, diapers, baby food, more diapers, and more baby food. We parents love our babies so much, yet there's so much to do!

It is possible to not answer the phone, to avoid returning messages, to ignore someone knocking at the door, and to avoid doing our e-mail, but most of us *cannot ignore our crying babies.* Baby cries awaken an archetypal drive in us to nurture, protect, and sustain our own. So, of course, with responding around the clock, we get sleep deprived, tired, and crabby. This is totally natural. It happens to all of us.

But what happens when we are sleep deprived and stressed for a long time? We can get mildly depressed. Apparently, sleep deprivation sometimes biologically results in depression even when there's nothing to be depressed about. For example, one study took healthy young childless volunteers and deprived them of deep sleep (found during delta-wave and dream stages) every night for a month. At the end of the month, they were evaluated. Every single one of them had become clinically and biologically depressed! And these young volunteers had no baby in the picture, no one crying to wake them up, and no one saying, "You get the baby, I'm tired."

Sleep deprivation also makes our daily hassles seem more intense. We feel worse, and we take things harder—like encountering rude people, waiting at red lights, or enduring long lines at the grocery store. When we're exhausted, we lose our sense of humor. We just can't cope as well.

In our relationships, we also feel more emotionally out of control. We think we hear something mean and snap! We crack back with something hostile. One minute we're laughing, and the next one, crying. And the fuse on our temper is only a millimeter long. Astoundingly, all of this is normal, given a few months of sleep deprivation and so much to do. It doesn't mean that our relationships are bad. It simply means that we're tired and going through a tremendous transition in our lives.

Then there's who-does-what to consider. For example, here are some of the tasks we new parents must divvy up and do.

- *The breakfast dishes*
- *The dinner dishes*
- *Setting the table*
- *Cleaning the counters*
- *Mopping the kitchen floor*
- *Dusting the house*
- *Vacuuming the house*

20

- *Cleaning the floors*
- *Cleaning the bathroom*
- *Cleaning out the garage*
- *Cleaning out the basement*
- *Shopping for Baby's needs*
- *Figuring out the other things we need to get*
- *Cooking dinner*
- *Making the other kids' lunches*
- *Making breakfast*
- *Taking out the garbage*
- *Sweeping outside*
- *Putting gas in the car*
- *Changing the oil in the car*
- *Changing lightbulbs in the house*
- *Washing the car*
- *Repairing the car*
- *Changing the baby's diapers*
- *Feeding the baby*
- *Getting up with the baby at night*
- *Getting the baby dressed in the morning*
- *Bathing the baby*
- *Playing with the baby*
- *Dealing with a crying baby*
- *Taking the children to their doctors' appointments*
- *Taking the children to school*
- *Making sure the kids have everything they need when they leave for the day*
- *Getting the baby or kids to sleep at night*
- *Making the bed(s)*

- *Doing the laundry*
- *Putting away the laundry*
- *Doing the grocery shopping*
- *Picking up medicines we need*
- *Cleaning up the yard*
- *Doing the weeding*
- *Taking the dog for a walk*
- *Changing the cat's litter box*
- *Making sure the doors and windows are locked at night*
- *Turning off all the lights when not needed*
- *Doing repair work around the house*
- *Helping the kids with homework*
- *Cleaning out the refrigerator*
- *Watering the plants*
- *Tidying up the common living areas*
- *Putting away the toys*
- *Calming the baby when he or she is upset*

Of course, this isn't everything. We once created a more complete list in order to help couples having a baby, but we found that our list of over six hundred items just depressed everybody even more. Not to mention the fact that most of us handle these chores while having to work part- or full-time, too. So it's no wonder that after our baby has come, we feel overwhelmed.

What else do we know? From sixteen studies that followed parents before and after babies arrived, we learned more.

- **Even though both parents are working much harder, they both feel unappreciated.**

- **During the first year after babies arrive, the frequency and intensity of relationship conflicts increase.**

• It is normal for a mom's sexual desire to drop precipitously after birth and even stay low for the first year, especially if she is nursing. Consequently, sex declines dramatically.

• Moms usually become very involved with their babies. But due to their fatigue, they have less to offer their partners emotionally.

• Both moms and dads undergo major changes in their own identities—for example, how they think of themselves not only as parents and partners, but also as friends, brothers, sisters, sons, and daughters. Their values may change, and their goals in life, too.

• Moms and dads often want to be better at parenting than their own parents were with them.

• Many couples change their relationship with time. They start to date events as "Before Baby" and "After Baby." Most important is when Baby did something for the first time.

• Right after the baby is born, many women close to new moms arrive to help out. But this society of women can crowd out the new dads. Dads often respond by withdrawing from their babies and working more, especially if there's more conflict at home.

• Babies withdraw emotionally from fathers who are unhappy with their relationship with their partners. But babies don't withdraw from unhappy moms. This withdrawal from dads can be tragic for babies.

If this is all that happened after we had babies, our birthrate might also precipitously decline. Fortunately, this isn't the whole story. Having a baby means experiencing those moments when our baby grabs our thumb and holds on for dear life. When we look at our baby's toes and they look like peas. And a month later, the toes grow and they look like string beans. Those moments when our baby's mouth curls up and she gives us her first smile. Or when he gurgles and laughs. Or when we gaze at each other as Baby falls softly asleep between us. Or when Baby flashes the world a grin from atop our shoulders. There's nothing better than taking our baby for a stroll on a warm summer's day. Or playing with a toy and watching our baby laugh.

Maybe the problem is that we have unrealistic expectations about what will happen after baby arrives. Dads expect that when babies come, moms will finally be happy, especially with them. New moms will feel fulfilled as women and see their husbands as manly and potent. They'll get turned on more easily and want to make love all the time. Meanwhile, moms expect that their men will finally open up emotionally and be more sensitive and loving. Their husbands will want to spend hours and hours just cuddling and listening to them. And they'll want to play with their babies, take care of their babies, and be close as a family all the time. So the first straw may look like this: She'll want to be held, but he'll want to put on the game; and later on, when he wants sex, she'll be tired and want to sleep. But there must be some way to navigate this transition into parenthood smoothly.

MANAGING CONFLICT

Most couples fight, especially when they're stressed and tired. It's natural. The secret to managing conflicts for new parents is to make the fights constructive, not destructive. Constructive means respectful, not disrespectful; gentle and not critical; and taking responsibility for our part and not being defensive. It means listening, not just broadcasting, and acknowledging our partner's point of view, not just repeating our own. Conflict can help us understand our partner better, but we have to be open to accepting our partner's influence and not insisting on getting our way.

If we disrespect each other during conflicts, conflicts become destructive; relationships are marked by criticism, defensiveness, the silent treatment, no compromise, no warmth, and no humor. Closeness spirals downhill fast. We wind up walking on eggshells, fighting louder, or withdrawing and avoiding one another. None of us wants that.

However, conflict managed well can lead us to deeper compassion for one another. Then we can be more of a team, cope better with our stress, and navigate this transition to parenthood with ease.

WHAT ABOUT INTIMACY?

Having a new baby means there's new sweetness in life—and more work to do. But when we're so busy, we forget to say "Thank you." Appreciation seems unnecessary. And we forget to ask, "How was your day?" Time for conversation disappears. If we get a chance to talk, we try—and get interrupted—in midsentence.

We don't experience each other's lives in the same consistent, close way that we did before the baby was born. Not being fully engaged makes intimacy so much more difficult. The increasing emotional demands that hamper intimacy are matched by the often different expectations that couples have about physical contact after the baby is born. Men may want and need physical intimacy to help feel close to their partners, while all women can think about is that they feel about as attractive as a potato.

Ellen Kreidman, in her book *Is There Sex After Kids?* tells the story of going to her obstetrician for her nine-month postpartum checkup. She asked her doctor about sex. She didn't tell him that she had been lacking sexual desire since the birth of the baby. She expected the doctor to tell her, "Sorry. No sex for the next two years." He examined her. Then he said, "You can resume sexual relations now." She was stunned. When she drove home with her husband, he asked her what her doctor had said. She replied, "The doctor said no sex for two years." He blanched. Then she said, "Not really . . . ," relieving him. But the reality was she wished that had been the doctor's assessment.

Ellen's story is not unusual. Sexual desire for many new moms seems to dry up, and they become much less emotionally available to their men. Faced with this lack of intimacy from their partners, men may withdraw from both their women and their babies. But during this transition time, it's crucial for husbands and wives to find the time to talk, to stay attuned to one another, and to reach out to one another. Sexual intimacy arises from emotional intimacy. And emotional intimacy comes from partners making the effort to find each other through the maze of duties to perform. When partners feel cherished and appreciated, affection comes naturally. It's no longer the last chore of the day. Then romance and passion can reawaken.

WE'RE BUILDING A LEGACY

The master couples in our studies sense that they are building something beyond their relationships, something bigger than themselves. With the arrival of their new babies, they are joining the flow of the generations. Now there are children to carry into the world their values, their visions, and their legacies. They ask themselves and each other, what do we want our legacies to be?

They examine everything with new eyes. What does it mean to have a home? Should we have mealtimes together, or apart? If one of us gets sick, how should we care for each other? And if we triumph, should we celebrate? What if we fail? Should we honor birthdays? What about the holidays? Should it be Christmas or Hanukkah? Kwanzaa or Ramadan? And our extended families? When should we include them? What about TV? Do we want it limited, or not? How about church? And when we vacation, should we do trips in the country, or in the city? What about our philosophy regarding emotions? Should we stay silent about our feelings, or say them out loud? There are so many ways for babies to learn what matters, and every family values thoughts, emotions, and experiences differently.

Each of us represents the family we've come from. And each of our families embodies a culture, that unique set of symbols, values, and rituals. When we become partners and new parents together, we merge not only our families but those cultures as well, and so we create a new culture together.

With our baby's arrival, we face a profound decision: From the cultures we've inherited and the new one we've created, what should we keep and transmit to our offspring, and what should we leave behind?

We can think about this decision and control what our babies absorb. Or we can avoid thinking about it, and let it just happen outside our awareness. Then we "vote with our feet"; in other words, we let our babies learn by what we do, regardless of whether we've thought about the consequences of our actions on our babies. Either way, by the daily choices we make we create a legacy for our children. Our master couples have shown us that by making these choices with purposeful awareness and intention, our children inherit the best from us.

Above all, there's the baby.

Our most important message is this:

The greatest gift you can give your baby is a happy and strong relationship between the two of you

Here's why.

Most babies suffer when there is relationship conflict between parents. Our studies and those of others have shown that parental irritability, hostility, and fighting lead to poor parent-child interaction. This in turn creates a dangerous emotional climate for babies.

For example, the blood pressures of babies rise when they witness or overhear their parents fighting. With parental alienation or depression, parents poorly coordinate face-to-face play with their babies and thereby confuse them. Unhappy parents also misread their babies' emotional cues and more often make wrong responses to them. Sometimes, they stop responding to their babies altogether. Overall, their interactions with their babies become more negative and less positive.

Just how serious is this? If babies can't talk, how do they know we're being hostile? Even if they do, can't they adapt to it? When they're so young, aren't they more resilient?

The answers are all no. We now know that even minor signs of untreated depression in parents have profound effects on babies. Infants of these parents often withdraw, at first just from fathers and later from mothers. They can also become depressed themselves, and less physically healthy. They are at greater long-term risk for developing emotional, cognitive, and behavioral problems.

The most troubling research finding we've learned is that parenting compromised by poor partner relationships nearly always has one effect. Compromised parenting will interfere with an infant's ability to self-regulate and to stay calm. Suppose an infant looks away because it is overstimulated and upset, and the baby's attempt to look away and calm down is not understood or respected by the parents. Some parents think that when the baby looks away from them, the baby doesn't like them. We've even seen parents in our lab forcibly move their infant's head so that the baby has to maintain eye contact with the parents. Then the infant is robbed of one of its main methods for self-soothing and adapting to the level of stimulation—looking away. The baby is forced to try a more extreme method of regulating the world, such as escalating his protests, or withdrawing.

During that instant, the baby has lost an opportunity to learn that with his behavior, he can affect his world. If that moment becomes characteristic of the parent-infant relationship, the baby will also learn that he can't communicate his emotions successfully and his emotions don't count. Doesn't that sound like what an unhappy couple might feel?

This issue is momentous because of what might fail to develop in the baby. In the first three years of life, fundamental neural processes are being laid down that have to do with the infant's ability to self-soothe, focus attention, trust in the love and nurturance of his parents, and emotionally attach to his mother and father. This means that a baby born to parents in an unhappy relationship might not develop the neural networks needed for school achievement, healthy peer relationships, and a future happy life.

These findings yell out to us that our babies need us to maintain healthy relationships with each other. When we savor each other, our babies rest in the cradle of our contentment.

SUMMARY

We couples are all in the same soup when a new baby arrives. The challenges, the stresses, the strong emotions, the hassles, the work, and the joys, too, are what we all get. But we can choose to either cope well with the challenges, or not. We won't eliminate the stresses. They're a natural part of becoming parents. But the good news is that we can stop thinking they are the fault of our partners, or the results of a bad relationship. By increasing that awareness and learning the ingredients for keeping our relationships healthy, we can nourish our babies with sweet food, and not sour milk.

2

DELIGHT IN YOUR BABY

During our study "Bringing Baby Home," we've had the pleasure of getting to know 222 babies. They've renewed our faith in humanity. Babies are amazing. We think they're tiny and helpless. But research reveals quite another story. When our babies are born, they are extremely competent, and so are we. And we are all are preset to respond to each other.

In the mid-1960s, scientists put babies under the microscope. And they were stunned. Here's what they learned: Forty-two minutes *after being born,* babies can mimic the facial expressions of an adult. This isn't just reflex, like a quick smile. Babies imitate the adult's internal experience, too, by re-creating the same physiological arousal pattern inside their bodies. This means babies are replicating the internal state of the adult. And in the first minutes after birth, if someone supports Baby's head, Baby will turn his or her head toward Mom's voice 100 percent of the time, and toward Dad's voice 80 percent of the time, rather than toward the doctor's voice. Within minutes, babies know where their bread is buttered!

Scientists find that if a particular visual image is shown to a hungry baby who is sucking on a nipple, over time the baby gets bored and habituated to the image. Baby keeps sucking but doesn't look at the image as much. But present a new image only a bit different from the first one, and Baby stops sucking for a moment. Her heart rate drops, and her eyes open wide in something like surprise. The baby has oriented to the new image. She's constructed a template of a visual image in her mind, and when it changes, she is surprised and suddenly keys into the new image. By watching for surprise in babies, scientists have learned what babies see—apples versus oranges.

Show a newborn a small moving red ball in the Brazelton Neonatal Behavioral Assessment for Newborns and she will follow the ball with her eyes, attentive and interested. But show her Mom's or Dad's face, and Baby will become excited, worked up, and entranced in a way that no ball could elicit. Baby's ready to play! And there's no way we parents can remain passive. We all want to engage.

Our babies want to interact with us from the moment they're born. And our face is a Picasso to them. In fact, for Baby there's no more exciting toy than our face. Nor is there any music more enchanting than our voice—Mozart included.

Studies also demonstrate how competent we are as parents instinctively, despite our worries. For example, intuitively we play with babies in a very special way. We raise our pitch when we talk and accentuate our words: "Niiiice babieee, prettieee babieee, what do you seeeeee, Babieee?" Babies love this, because higher pitch is easier to hear, and exaggerated enunciation teaches them sounds and words. We also take turns with babies in face-to-face play, doing a delicate, intricate dance. And our games evolve over time, unfolding new leaves of complexity as they change.

Of all the faces we make, there are five that most intrigue babies when we're face-to-face. First, our mock-surprise face: We open our eyes wide, raise our eyebrows, open our mouths, and . . . hold it. We say something like "Ahhhh-hhhh," with our pitch going up. Second, our smile: We give a big, broad, genuine grin that crinkles our eyes at the corners. Third, our frown: We lower our brows, draw them together, and say something like "Aaooohhh," lowering our pitch at the end of the "ooohhh" part. Fourth, we make the "Oh, poor baby" empathy face that combines mock surprise with a frown. And fifth, we just look neutral. Babies love these faces.

On the other hand, babies hate a stonelike face. Psychologist Edward Tronick tried an experiment called "the Still Face." Moms or dads were asked to stare at their three-month-old babies and not make a single move or sound. Tronick discovered that most babies perform the same preset routines to engage their still-faced parent. They coyly look away. Then they may smile, coo, cock their heads, or look up. If these fail to melt parents into responding, they whimper, fuss, and may even cry. Our babies need us to be fluid, not frozen.

By six weeks of age, our babies gaze at us for longer periods of time with big, wide eyes. Pediatricians say their eyes "brighten." At last, they're really connecting with us. And by their twelfth week, they no longer have to be eight inches from our face to see us (about the distance from face to nipple). They track us while we're moving around the room. And they shine that long-distance smile on us like sunrise.

At around six months, they shift again—this time, to objects. Now they want to play with us and everything else, too. They've cognitively leaped into the world around them. They coax both parents simultaneously into playing with them through a smile for Dad, then another for Mom.

We met a baby named Regina in Lausanne, Switzerland. She could've won a peace prize. Her parents were leagues apart to begin with. But six-month-old Regina enveloped Mom and Dad with her joy. She'd engage one parent in play, then look at the other parent and smile, inviting the outside parent into the game. Soon, the couple laughed not only with her but with each other. In time, their marital happiness flowered. Maybe Regina had something to do with this. If so, she was the youngest family therapist ever.

CHILDREN AND TIME

There are two things that are very different about children, compared to adults. First, children are on a very different time scale than adults. Everything happens more slowly for children. They need time to react, time to process what is going on. When Mom sticks her tongue out at her newborn, Baby will respond by imitating the expression. But Mom may have to wait as long as forty seconds to see that little tongue point out. Usually, we're too busy to notice Baby's responses to us. We have to downshift to first before playtime. If we turn off the phone, turn off the TV, and slow way, way down, it will enhance our lives, and Baby's, too.

Second, kids are much better than us at being in the moment, fully engaged and present. Unlike us, their attention is not in ten different places at once. They're not planning their shopping list. They don't need an agenda. There's no task to accomplish. They're not even building their résumé. They're with us, right now.

If we can put on the brakes, stop multitasking, and just enjoy our babies, imagine the pleasure. And our babies will love it, too. They'll feel seen by us, because we'll have taken the time to know them.

A BRIEF HISTORY OF PREGNANCY AND CHILDBIRTH

Not so long ago, the thought of enjoying our children would've seemed blasphemous. Children were literally "to be seen, not heard," as the old adage goes. Actually, it was worse than that. From the moment they were in the womb, they weren't even to be seen. Here's what we mean.

Until recently, pregnant women were shunned in society. These days, that may surprise us, as our magazine covers glow with pictures of pregnant movie stars. But as late as the 1950s, pregnant women were forbidden from entering schools. It was considered unseemly and disgusting for kids to see pregnant women, because they would be reminded of sex. Never mind that every day many kids were returning home to mothers pregnant with their siblings-to-be. Following suit, CBS would not allow the word "pregnant" to be used on TV. Lucille Ball was the first pregnant woman to be spotlighted. Her skits of being huge with baby and unable to get up off a couch to answer a doorbell are hilarious. However, it was her determination to show her pregnancy and her courage fighting the network that made it possible for America to witness a pregnant star on TV. And Lucy wasn't pretending—she really was pregnant.

In those days, medical professionals in the industrialized world treated pregnant women with detachment, too. Childbirth was depersonalized, and pregnancy was portrayed as an illness. Child development professor Sharon Heller writes, "Hospital; male doctor; C-section; epidural; Pitocin; episiotomy—outside the industrialized world, these terms would not suggest [the nature of] childbirth." Of course, medical progress maximized survival for both mother and baby. But these advances came at a cost. Birth was dealt with matter-of-factly, with technological precision. Open the car hood; remove the carburetor.

The Monty Python film *The Meaning of Life* contains a skit in which two surgically gowned obstetricians discuss all the complicated medical equipment in the delivery room, including a machine that simply goes "beep." The head of hospital inspects the room, making sure they have the machine that goes beep. Everything's all set. But wait a minute; where's the woman? Still out in the hall, moaning on a gurney. Oops.

Heller wrote that modern medicine "should have made childbirth less anxious, but it didn't. To feel safe, human beings need the comfort of others." But that profound truth was ignored until Marshall Klaus and John Kennel's study, conducted in the 1970s. Here's what the two physicians stumbled upon.

Klaus and Kennel always ordered their medical student assistants to usher women in labor through the usual impersonal hospital routine. But one of the students, bless his heart, didn't follow instructions. He stayed with the moms and gave them comfort and emotional support. At first, Klaus and Kennel were furious with him. Then they looked at his data. They noticed that the moms he cared for were doing much better than the other moms. It wasn't that he was a magician. He was just using methods of compassion during childbirth that doulas had been practicing for centuries. (Doulas are women who have traditionally provided emotional support for women during labor and delivery.) Swiftly, the two physicians modified their hospital's childbirth procedures to include doulas. Then they documented how pregnant women fared with doulas by their side. Their findings blew apart our assumptions about medical "progress."

There's an old saying that goes "New friends are silver, but old friends are gold." Perhaps that's true of certain healing traditions, too. Here's what Klaus and Kennel found when doulas were involved in labor and delivery: a 60 percent drop in requests for epidural blocks, a 25 percent decrease in the length of labor, a 30 percent drop in the use of pain medication, a 40 percent decrease in the use of forceps, less postpartum depression, a 50 percent drop in C-sections, a 40 percent decline in the use of oxytocin to increase contractions, and far less pain during labor. In the group of moms with no doula, 63 percent of the babies developed feeding problems after birth. In the group with doulas, only 16 percent of the babies later had feeding problems. Modern methods may help, but good old-fashioned emotional support helps, too. Doulas have an impact, for the better.

What is the bottom line here? If a professional treats a pregnant woman coldly and roughly, both she and the baby will suffer. If s/he supports the mother with touch, comfort, reassurance, empathy, affection, respect, and love, they are both more likely to flourish.

This lesson applies not only for mothers and their newborns, but for all parents and children. But again, this knowledge has been hard to come by in the medical world.

WHAT DO BABIES NEED? AND PARENTS?

The history of medical child care is not a pretty one. It's been an attempt at care, but until recently an ill-informed one. For example, not long ago, parents were banned from visiting their sick and hospitalized children. They couldn't see or hold them, even if their children were upset or crying. It was standard medical practice to isolate kids. Even nurses and doctors were told, "Hands off." Sounds draconian, doesn't it?

But here's the care behind this bear: Early in the twentieth century, infections raged in hospitals. Medical professionals tried everything they knew. But in those days, there were no antibiotics, vaccines, pasteurized milk, or chlorinated water. Doctors' efforts were hopeless. Both inside and outside hospitals, children died at an alarming rate. Between 1850 and 1900, one out of four children died before the age of five, most during infancy. Only after 1946 did penicillin finally slow the onslaught.

In the late 1920s, doctors were at their wits' end. Quarantine was all they could think of to stop contagions. For better or for worse, it worked. Sequestering kids in hospitals became the answer.

At the same time, the writings of psychologist John Watson grabbed the spotlight. Watson was president of the American Psychological Association. In the 1930s, he raised his fist from his supposedly scientific pulpit and preached "tough love." The instinct of a mother to caress her children unconditionally was evil, he proclaimed. His teachings echoed the biblical adage "Spare the rod and spoil the child." Parents who hugged and touched their kids were creating dependent, clingy, horrible monster children. And by breeding America's future criminals, they were precipitating society's downfall.

For the sake of America, parents needed to stop touching their babies and older kids. Instead of "spoiling" them (Watson coined the term), raise them with reason, discipline, and self-control, he said. *The Wife's Handbook,* a publication of the time, defined "spoiling" as picking up a crying baby or allowing it to fall asleep in parental arms. So *never* pick up a crying baby, Watson counseled. Deny those instincts. And never let a baby fall asleep while being cradled. Later, if a child really excelled at something, be meager with praise. A pat on the head should do. Tough love.

Hospitals loved Watson. His ideas could be used to bludgeon

parents away from their sick children, whose kisses just spread germs. In the 1940s, as journalist and social activist Deborah Blum writes, it was standard policy to let parents visit their sick kids only *one hour a week!*

It worked, to some degree. When kids were isolated, infections diminished. Infant and child mortality decreased. Watson was proclaimed a hero. Everywhere, doctors urged parents to listen to Watson. Stop touching the children, even if the kids weren't sick. Stop picking them up and holding them, regardless of whether they were hurt and upset. It was wrongheaded.

Because after a while, doctors noticed an ugly new problem. In quarantine, many children improved temporarily. Then their condition plummeted, out of nowhere. Or slowly they became silent, listless, and withdrawn. They stopped smiling. They just quietly withered away. For no known medical reason, children were dying in hospitals again.

Quarantine's dark face may have stayed hidden if not for World War II. When the Nazis started to bomb London, seven hundred thousand children were evacuated. In the countryside, they stayed with other adults, bomb free and well treated.

A psychiatrist named John Bowlby, however, noticed that these kids were also quietly wilting, just like children quarantined in hospitals. Bowlby asserted that they were grief-stricken due to separation from their mothers. This was a radical idea. But nobody listened to Bowlby. He was viewed as overly sentimental and unscientific, unlike Watson (who, in reality, had no science behind him, either).

It wasn't until after World War II that John Bowlby and Mary Ainsworth did some research to prove they were right. They observed how children responded to brief separations from their mothers and reunions. Some babies were securely attached; that is, they missed their moms when they left, and felt comforted when they returned. This indicated a healthy relationship between mother and child. But some children were far less secure. They either acted (1) "avoidant," indifferent to their mother's return, or

(2) "anxious-ambivalent," meaning that they were so upset about the separation that at reunion they still couldn't be comforted.

Then scientists found that the latter "insecure attachment" patterns hurt children's later adjustment. As teens and adults, they were a mess psychologically. In contrast, "securely attached" children were more resilient and better adjusted in later years. They were more independent, and they explored their world more than insecurely attached children. This research put Bowlby's observations on a solid scientific footing. Secure attachment was a quality of relationship, not a quality of the baby. Without it, children might suffer for a lifetime.

The 1950s brought more news. At the University of Wisconsin, a psychologist named Harry Harlow began working with baby rhesus macaque monkeys. He conducted a profoundly dramatic series of studies on the importance of mothers' love. Thanks to Bowlby and Ainsworth, other psychologists now knew a baby's attachment to its mother was important. But they claimed that mother's milk was the glue that linked baby to mother. All babies needed was nurturance with food. Babies so young weren't capable of emotionally connecting with others. The nipple was it for them. Harlow, however, brilliantly proved otherwise.

In his experiments, he gave baby monkeys a vital choice. They could spend time with a surrogate "mother" constructed of wire that had a nipple and gave milk when the baby sucked. Or they could spend time with a soft terry-cloth surrogate "mother" that only gave what Harlow called "contact comfort," but no milk. The babies chose the cloth mother, not the milk-producing wire mother. Furthermore, when frightened, babies ran to the cloth mother, not the cold wire mother. Baby monkeys with a cloth mother were also much better adjusted than those with a cold, wire mother, despite having all the milk they wanted.

This solid scientific research pointed to only one conclusion: Babies and children need the unbridled affection, comfort, love, and support that mothers can instinctively provide.

We now know that many of the children quarantined in hospitals actually died not from their diseases, but from depression and intense loneliness. These children were touch deprived. They were starved for affection—and died from not having it.

Watson was dead wrong, and his advice was harmful, even fatal. Unfortunately, his work affected every American institution focused on children and parenting.

Watson's teachings have stuck like sap to this day. In every public talk we give, parents agonize: They are "spoiling" their babies by picking them up when they cry, or holding and comforting them when they've fallen down. They are giving in to their babies' "manipulation." They know they should follow a contemporary pediatrician's advice and just let Baby cry himself to sleep alone. But they just can't do it.

Neither could we with our baby.

Through research, we now know our parental instincts are right, and this idea of "spoiling" babies is misguided. We reassure parents that when a baby cries, it's simply sending out an SOS. If we ignore our baby's crying, we are teaching our baby that the world is a place that won't respond to his message. We cannot spoil a baby by responding to him. Our emotional availability and responsiveness to his emotional cues are the most effective ways of creating independence and resilience in him.

TOUCH BABIES AND CHILDREN, TOUCH ONE ANOTHER

Unwanted touch is a problem at any age, with any person. We are not advocating touching adults or children when contact is unwelcome. Unfortunately, scandals of sexual harassment and child molestation have hit the front pages, and the crimes of a few have negatively affected the many. Preschool and elementary school administrators now typically warn their staff to not touch students even when a child is injured.

Yet as we've seen, infants and children crave physical comfort when they are upset. Verbal soothing is great, but young ones respond better to touch. Psychologist Tiffany Field scientifically tested sixty variations of verbal comfort and sixty forms of physical comfort. She found that only three of the verbal phrases actually comforted young children, while fifty-three of the physical forms of comfort worked well.

Field developed infant massage techniques after she had a premature child. In her day, parents were forbidden to touch their prematurely born babies. Born tiny and kept in a plastic incubator, they looked as if they'd break if touched. But Field instinctively knew better, and proved it later in her research. She showed that when parents were taught infant massage techniques and massaged their babies for just fifteen minutes a day, the babies' body weight increased 47 percent in ten days. Babies with no massage gained weight much more slowly. Massaged preemies were also able to leave the hospital sooner, were healthier, and were more closely bonded with their parents than nonmassaged babies. Over ninety studies have been conducted to date, and they all demonstrate the benefits of massage for children.

It is remarkable to see a baby being massaged. The baby is like a cat, purring, happy, and relaxed. Another vital way of connecting emotionally with Baby is through face-to-face play.

THE IMPORTANCE OF
FACE-TO-FACE PLAY WITH YOUR BABY

One of the best lessons babies learn in face-to-face play with us is that the world (and we are the baby's world at that moment) will respond and not ignore their wishes. We can do our best parenting if we:

- *Stay emotionally warm and available.*
- *Stay responsive to our baby's cues.*

Because of their immature nervous systems, it's easy for babies to become too stimulated. They're like sensitive antennae. With too many signals, they'll just hear static. And we all know how aversive that is. At those times, babies try to tune out the stimulation they're getting, so they can reset their dials and tune in again. They may turn their heads away from us, not because they dislike us, but because they need to withdraw in order to calm down. After a while, they normally turn back toward us. They may also try to soothe themselves by sucking on something, like their hand or a toy. Through tuning in, and then tuning out or self-soothing, they attempt to regulate their response to stimuli.

Babies also need our support to self-regulate. So what happens when we don't respect our baby's looking away and we try to force her to stay tuned in to us? We rob our baby of one of the main ways she has for calming down. Then Baby may whimper, fuss more, and eventually full-out scream her distress. Baby is learning that she can't control her world, and, worse, that the people in her world don't care about her discomfort. If that happens once or twice, it's no big deal. Especially if we parents see that a repair is needed in our response and we make one. But if we frequently block our baby from turning away and self-soothing, then our baby will have no choice but to withdraw. Baby will be learning that the only way to handle hardship is to turn away from everyone and everything. None of us wants our baby to learn that lesson.

There's even more at stake. Research has shown that during the first three years of life, fundamental neural structures are being built that have to do with Baby's self-soothing, his ability to focus attention, his trust in his parents' love and nurturance, and the security of his attachment to his mother and father. In other words, Baby's experiences of parental respect and love are literally laying down patterns of brain tissue that will dictate Baby's future responses to the world.

When we experience emotion, it is reflected in the activity of the frontal lobes of our brain. Brain-wave research has demonstrated that when people experience emotions related to withdrawal, like sadness, fear, or disgust, their right frontal lobe lights up like a theater on Broadway. But when people experience emotions related to engaging with the world, like interest, amusement, affection, happiness, and anger, their left frontal lobe fires up. This laterality is true of babies, too. Psychologists Nathan Fox and Richard Davidson discovered that if babies are awake, relaxed, and typically more active in the right frontal brain, they'll cry when their mother leaves the room. But if they're typically more left-brain active, they'll be fine when their mother leaves the room. In other words, whether they're normally more active on the right or the left frontal brain predicts whether they'll respond to changes in their world with sadness (a withdrawal emotion) or happily continued play (emotional engagement with the world).

Studies also show that depressed people have more brain-wave activity in the right frontal lobe of the brain. They process everyday experience with "withdrawal" emotions. In contrast, nondepressed people have more brain-wave activity in the left frontal lobe, and they involve themselves more in the world.

The message here is profound: how we answer our baby's cries and how we also play with her is cementing in place Baby's attitude toward her future world. Ignore our baby now and it's likely she'll learn to withdraw later, perhaps into a cocoon of depression. Respond to Baby now and she'll most likely stay engaged with her world.

In our longitudinal research, we discovered that face-to-face play with Baby affects Baby's later response to the world, too. When both parents are simpatico in their play, Baby has the most fun, and so do we parents. This play predicts a positive outcome for Baby. On the other hand, there are two pokers that can pop Baby's balloon and ruin her fun—and ours.

The first is uncoordinated play between parents. When we parents compete for Baby's attention instead of joining together to play the same game, Baby seems to hate it. One parent may suddenly withdraw from the play, or swoop in and cut off the other parent. In response, Baby may arch her back, frown, cry, or, in baby language, seem to yell, "This is messing me up. Knock it off!"

The second balloon buster for Baby is being overstimulated. When we parents are ignoring Baby's cues that say, "*No!* I don't want to do this!" Baby may signal this subtly at first, but if she's ignored, she'll turn up the volume. If "No" still doesn't work, she'll just plain withdraw. That's not good. We've lost connection with Baby.

But what's a parent to do? Baby doesn't speak yet. So how can we know when Baby's getting frazzled and needs some downtime?

SIGNALS THAT BABY IS OVERSTIMULATED

As we watched babies playing with their parents, we witnessed how babies say to their parents, "Give me a break for a minute or two!" Here are the signals they give when they need to self-soothe.

• **LOOKING AWAY.** This signal can be very clear, with the baby turning her head away, or it can be simply looking from our face to our less-stimulating shirt.

• **SHIELDING FACE WITH HANDS.** Babies will put their hands in front of their face and look like they are trying to shield themselves.

• **PUSHING AWAY.** When the baby is more coordinated, he may push a toy or other object away to show that he doesn't want to play with it.

• **CLEARLY WRINKLED FOREHEAD.** When the medial (middle, above the nose) portion of a baby's forehead is bunched up (that is as much wrinkling as is possible with all the baby fat in the face), it means she is getting upset, often because she is overstimulated. The forehead makes the baby look like she is sad, or angry. However, when the baby's forehead gets only slightly wrinkled, as though there is a butterfly on her forehead, this is usually not a negative sign and means she is concentrating.

- **ARCHING THE BACK.** One sign that a baby is upset is that she arches her back and tenses her body.

- **FUSSING.** The baby's voice starts what seems like the beginning of crying and protesting.

- **SHOWING A MIXTURE OF EMOTION,** such as the baby's expression going back and forth between joy and fear.

- **CRYING.** There are levels of upset in the crying of babies. The baby may eventually build up to a cry in which there is about a second of "winding up" intake of breath. Then the baby really hauls off and lets out a cry that is loud, shrill, and painful to hear. This is called a Valsalva cry. In a Valsalva cry, the lungs are working against a resistance, like when we blow up a stiff balloon, or lift a heavy weight. It is very stressful for the baby. For example, the baby's blood pressure will increase, and the number of white blood cells in the baby's blood will increase.

WHAT TO DO: REPAIRING OVERSTIMULATION

Overstimulation is not always bad for our baby. In fact, it's one way that our baby "stretches" emotionally and cognitively, increasing her range of comfort and creating more complex mental structures.

But, in general, we should try to be sensitive when our babies are overstimulated. The key to repairing our interaction with our baby is to be calm and let the baby take the break he or she needs. Once Baby is calm and looks ready to engage, we can gently call her attention back to us and resume our interaction. To repair the interaction, we need to back off, let our baby look away, and see if she can self-soothe. If Baby hasn't developed this skill yet, we can give her a helping hand (literally) by giving her something to suck, like our finger or a pacifier. We can also pick up Baby and hold her against the left side of our chest, where Baby can hear our heart. We can gently rock Baby and speak or sing softly to her. All of these will help Baby to be soothed, teach her in turn how to self-soothe, and show her that those in her world care about her. In sum, here's what we can do.

- STAY CALM. When we are calm, and are talking calmly and acting calmly, it helps the baby to calm herself.

- LET THE BABY SUCK ON SOMETHING.

- HOLD OUR BABY CLOSE. Touch the baby soothingly.

- SOFTEN OUR VOICE (while the baby recovers).

- When the baby looks at us again, continue with the play action or song in a softer, less-stimulating way that allows the baby to look away and recover.

- TRY IMITATING BABY. Doing exactly what Baby is doing will fascinate her.

- ATTUNEMENT. Here's a twist on imitation. Babies love it when we imitate them in a different way than they are acting. For example, if Baby is banging a spoon in a rhythm, we can imitate that rhythm with our voice. This will really catch Baby's interest.

Baby can signal that he is ready to interact with us again in a variety of ways.

- BABY LOOKS BACK AT US OR THE TOY WE ARE PLAYING WITH (this is a clear signal from a baby).

46

- **CALM FACE AND BREATHING.** When Baby has been able to calm his or her face and appears to be breathing fairly normally, he may be ready to be gently invited back to the play.

- **RELAXED BODY.** Baby's body has relaxed.

THINGS *NOT* TO DO

When we realize that our baby is getting fussy or looking away, we're tempted to just try harder by changing the game or increasing the intensity of the play. Unfortunately, our babies usually dislike this—it overstimulates them even more. The classic mistakes we parents can make are included in the following list. Remember now, it is not a tragedy if we find ourselves doing these things. It just means it's repair time. Here are the "don'ts."

- DON'T move your face in front of the baby's face wherever she moves her head (this does not allow the baby to look away and take the break she needs).

- DON'T move your face too close to your baby's face, such that it is difficult for her to look away.

- DON'T increase the pace of play or increase stimulation *after* your baby has given you a signal that she is overstimulated.

- DON'T switch back and forth between activities quickly *after* your baby has given you a signal that she is overstimulated (such as going quickly from a peekaboo game to a zooming game to a song with actions).

- DON'T physically move the baby's torso so that she is looking at you. Again, this doesn't allow the baby to look away and calm down, and babies usually don't like being physically constrained.

• DON'T stimulate the baby further by doing things like poking her or repeatedly wiping her mouth. Our mouths have a great many nerves in them, and stimulation of the mouth is especially arousing to a baby.

Babies and young children are completely fascinated by play. Play is an adventure. It isn't a chore. There is nothing to accomplish. It unfolds over time, and there is no right way to play. It is OK for us to be silly, to sing, to dance, to make funny mouth sounds, to touch and caress our baby, to blow spit bubbles, to tickle, to play peekaboo and "I'm gonna get you," to make blowing kissing sounds on Baby's tummy, and anything else.

The great news is that we parents don't have to be perfect. Good-enough parenting is terrific! In fact, playing with a baby is a lot like the sport of baseball. A great batting average in baseball is .300, which means the batter is actually making an out 70 percent of the time. In communication between moms and babies, psychologist Edward Tronick found that in play between three-month-old babies and their moms, miscoordination happened 70 percent of the time. Just like baseball! The moms who noticed the miscoordination and tried to repair it had babies that at one year old were happy and securely attached to them. So the key is repair. We can do our best, and then make repairs when we blow it.

Remember, the most powerful things we can do as parents are:

- *Stay warm and emotionally available.*
- *Stay responsive to Baby's cues.*

3

COOL DOWN YOUR CONFLICTS

We look on as a young family snuggles in the family room together, bathing in the glow of their new baby. The TV is on, and he's got the remote. Softly, she says, "Dear, would you please stop channel surfing?" He queries, "Why? I just want to see what's on. Maybe there's a good movie." Still sweetly, she replies, "But honey, it's too much stimulation. Let's settle on one show, OK?"

"But I don't like any of these shows. I want to keep looking."

"Does it really matter?" Then she whines, "Come on, just leave it on this one."

A chill cools the air. Now look at what happens next.

HE: Fine. OK, fine!

She: The way you say "Fine"—it's like you're saying "Shut up."

HE: I am not saying "Shut up." You're just being emotional.

She: I am *not* being emotional. I know that tone. You snap at me like I'm one of your employees. I don't appreciate being talked to like that.

HE: And I don't appreciate being nagged. Just leave me alone.

She: Screw you! If I didn't nag, you'd ignore me!

HE: Stop screaming! Talk about emotional? Why can't you control yourself?

She: Impossible with a jerk like you around!

The baby begins to fuss.

HE: Now look what you've done!

She: From the start, it's a fight with you. I stay calm and you blow up.

HE: No, you're a rattlesnake. One wrong move and you strike.

She: Why wouldn't I strike at somebody trying to trample me?

The baby squinches up her face, bears down for a heartbeat, then wails out her panic.

These two are sparring like boxers in a ring, dancing around in circles. No one takes responsibility. It's throw a jab here, block another one there, and counter with a left hook. Each partner feels blameless and sees the other as causing their own negativity. Over time the attacks get dirtier, and soon we've got brass knuckles in the gloves. That's when the big hurts come out.

It's easy to have fights like this when we're exhausted, stressed, and overwhelmed. They pop up out of nowhere, and over nothing. We anguish over them, especially when our babies witness us spiraling out of control. They watch us, absorbing it like a sponge.

Baby's arrival doesn't inspire new issues to fight over. In fact, most themes grappled with by couples remain static, from age twenty to age eighty. For example, this couple's fight mirrors what we have seen in our lab. Like 21 percent of our couples, these folks are duking it out over *how* they fight, not *what* they're fighting about. Most of us have this kind of fight.

It's about process, not content. The underlying issue gets swept away by our indignation at how we are being treated. We claw at each other about how our conflicts blow up, how we're torn apart by our partner's attacks, and how we end up as enemies, not allies. We rail about being taken for granted, pacified, or shut out altogether. In other words, we argue about how we've just danced, not which music to choose.

So, in our lab, we identified the *process* of the fight as the number one issue. But what really intrigued us was how the masters of the transition to parenthood managed their conflicts. Somehow they fought over the same issues, but differently. They were gentler, funnier, and kinder. Even though they might explode with anger, their words were less like knives and more like declarations of their rights. Let's imagine a replay of the previous couple if they'd been like our master couples.

She: Honey, would you mind not channel surfing? It's making me dizzy.

HE: Ah, come on, honey. You know I like to see what might be on. And we've got only 128 more channels to check.

She: OK. Well, I think I'll go scrub the kitchen floor.

HE: Trying the old guilt trip again, huh?

She: It's not working?

HE: You really hate me channel surfing that much?

She: Really. My head is so tired. It's just too much stimulation. It starts to hurt my eyes after a while.

HE: I didn't know that. Well, how about if we settle on the game?

She: Honey!

HE: Just thought I'd try. OK. What do you want to see?

She: How about the channel with the old movies. I love the romance.

HE: Gaaak.

She: OK, OK. What?

HE: I know. That Clint Eastwood flick on 44.

She: For you, anything.

This conversation smoothes out the dance. There's a complaint, but this time no blaming, criticism, or contempt. Nobody gets defensive, and nobody throws any punches. It's easier, lighter, and simpler. She states what she needs, he responds with his own needs, and she's more insistent in a playful way. He hangs in there and listens more seriously, and she restates her need, with more of her real feelings this time. He hears it, softens, and tries a weak attempt at a compromise bent his way. She stands her ground and says no dice. He's a little frustrated, and puts the ball in her court. She slam-dunks it her way. Then it's no way for him. Finally, they find common ground, and it's over. Eastwood saves the day. But really, it's their gentleness and willingness to hear one another and tango closer and closer to that center circle that does it. They dip in the middle.

Seem impossible? Not at all! When we watched these masters on videotape and analyzed what they were doing, a hundredth of a second at a time, the miracle of their dance appeared. All of our master couples were following the same steps. Even when they were furious and made a misstep, their quick repairs ushered them back into the dance.

We've talked about the lessons we learned from couples like these in our four earlier books, *Why Marriages Succeed or Fail* (1994), *The Seven Principles for Making Marriage Work* (1999), *The Relationship Cure* (2001), and *Ten Lessons to Transform Your Marriage* (2006). Yet we can never repeat them often enough. And they apply just as well to us today.

Let's return to couples like these through our mics and cameras. We've translated their steps into a simple recipe to follow. The ingredients aren't hard. We can all do this. The following chapters will describe each one for you.

There's one caveat, however, that we need to add. It's important that our babies not witness our fights. As we've seen, babies are profoundly affected by our fights in front of them, especially if those fights are savage. The last thing we want is to hurt our babies. So right off, here's a remedy.

Have a problem-solving meeting time. We shouldn't bring up issues if we think they'll lead to World War III. We need to talk about those privately. Some of our masters have weekly meeting times when the complaints and big issues come out. It works best if we each bring up one issue, not the long litany.

Don't discuss problems at mealtime. Fights during meals give us indigestion. And they may give our kids eating disorders later.

We can talk about a minor disagreement in front of our kids once they are about four years old. But they need to see us resolve the problem, too. It they're between four and eight years old, they love to see us hug or kiss after a squabble. Other endings won't make as much sense to them. We can also say a few words to explain what just happened. For example:

"Bobby, can we tell you what just happened? We got angry at each other, but then we talked about it. I listened to Mommy's feelings, and she listened to mine. That way, we could understand each other. Then we could work it out and make peace again."

If we slip up and a bad fight happens in front of the kids, more repairs are needed. Babies need to be comforted and held. If at all possible, holding the baby between us both is best, but only if there's peace between us. If there's still some tension, one of us needs to take the baby aside for cuddling while our partner gets some space. We'll go into this in more detail in a later chapter.

If our kids are older, we face different problems. They will be terrified that we're going to split up. We need to tell them that we won't (unless, of course, we plan to—that's a subject for a different book). Their other terror is that this fight is all their fault. Young children believe that they anchor the universe. Their brains haven't matured enough yet to allow them to witness the world as separate, and spinning in its own orbit. Therefore, whatever happens around them must have something to do with them. As adults, we know that's not true, but they don't. So we need to tell them very clearly that our fight had nothing to do with them, and that we love them. We can say that all parents argue from time to time because they have different opinions about things, and it's OK. Then we need to reassure them that we'll work out our differences, and we need to apologize to them for upsetting them. Last, we need to give them a hug, and make sure that our next conversation occurs outside the hearing of their beloved ears.

Now, with this caveat in mind, let's continue. We've listed the recipe our master couples follow to make sure their conflicts yield bread and not famine. Here are their ingredients for healthy conflict management.

- *Soften how you start the discussion.*
- *Accept influence by recognizing there are two valid viewpoints.*
- *Calm down by physiological self-soothing.*
- *Compromise.*
- *Process and understand the fight later, after you've calmed down.*
- *Figure out the conversation you needed to have, instead of the fight.*
- *Move from "gridlock" to "dialogue" when you face unsolvable problems, using the "dreams-within-conflict" method.*

Now we'll describe the essence of these ingredients in our next chapters.

4
SOFTEN HOW YOU
BRING UP A PROBLEM

James stretches out on the bed. It's 4 a.m. and he's wide awake. Next to him lie Baby Anna and little Joanie, who's three. On the far edge of the bed, Carrie, his wife, is sacked out. It's been a rough night. Anna was teething and cried. Joanie heard her, woke up, and came into the bed. Carrie is knocked out from caring for them both. But the only one awake is James. He reminisces: Remember what it was like when there was just the two of us, those long, gorgeous nights? Remember the hot tub? When was the last time we made love? Like six months ago?

Now he's getting upset. It's not fair! Why doesn't she pay attention to me anymore? The kids are great, but geez, there's gotta be a limit. It's always the kids. Never me. I wonder if she still wants me . . . I miss her.

The next morning, they slump over the kitchen table. James raises the issue. Tentatively, he says, "Carrie?"

"What?" she snaps back.

"Never mind," he grumbles. He rises and heads for the living room.

Turning to face him, Carrie adds, "I'm sorry, I'm just pooped . . . What is it?"

James mutters, "I miss you . . . I wish we could have a date one of these nights."

Carrie shakes her head. "How can we possibly go out on a date?

I've got to stay with Anna, especially now. She's miserable with those teeth coming in."

James persists. "I know. But I really miss you. Maybe I just miss us. We haven't had private time in so long, and every time when I think, 'Tonight's the night,' the kids get up and that's the end of it. I don't want to go on like this forever."

"Neither do I," Carrie reassures him. "I miss you, too. I don't know what to tell you."

"How about you still find me incredibly sexy and manly and you want to make mad love to me?"

"OK. I find you gorgeous and sexy, and I still love you. But can you wait awhile for the follow-through? Let's just get by this one tooth of Annie's, OK? Then I'll call my mom to come over and we'll have a date."

"Great."

In contrast, if this couple was less skilled, here's how that conversation could have sounded.

JAMES: Carrie, I need to talk.

CARRIE: What?

JAMES: We never have sex anymore, and I'm tired of it. You're not a woman anymore. You're just a mom. Kids, kids, kids . . . You're one of those mothers who spoils her kids rotten.

CARRIE: What are you talking about? Just because you can't connect to the kids doesn't mean I shouldn't. Joanie is three years old and the baby is just six months old. Who are they supposed to turn to? You? (*She laughs mockingly.*)

JAMES: You jump and come running every time they cry and they'll hang on to your apron strings forever. You're ruining those kids.

Notice how the real issue of wanting private time for the two of them darted underground? Which marriage would you rather be in?

The couple the first time around added an essential ingredient to their mix.

SOFTENED START-UP

"Start-up" refers to how we bring up an issue with our partner. In contrast, the couple in the second go-round began with a harsh start-up. The difference between the two methods makes all the difference. We discovered that the way a conflict conversation goes is determined by how it starts 96 percent of the time.

When we introduce an issue with harsh start-up, one of us blames the other, usually with criticism or contempt. In response, the other partner gets defensive and critical right back. Anger bubbles up, then skyrockets. No problems are resolved. In contrast, when softened start-up is used, no one gets blamed. Instead, one of us begins with a complaint. A complaint states what we *feel* about a situation, and the situation is described *neutrally*, not like a shot across the bow. Next, we state what we *do* need, not what we don't need. Softened start-ups are easier on the ears. They don't hurt us the way harsh start-ups do.

Most of the time harsh start-ups include what we call "the Four Horsemen of the Apocalypse." In our research, we discovered that these behaviors were our strongest predictors of relationship demise, especially if couples failed to repair them. When couples' problem-solving discussions contained these toxic behaviors repeatedly and couples had no antidotes for them, their relationships were not long for this world. So it's important that we understand these horsemen to keep them from trampling our relationships.

• CRITICISM is a way of complaining that globally attacks our partner's personality by pointing out his or her defects. When words like "lazy," "slob," "thoughtless," or "careless" pop up in our vocabulary, we know we're being critical. More subtle criticisms are phrases like "You never" or "You always." When we utter "always" or "never" about our partner, we're most likely enumerating our partner's inadequacies; for example, "You never clean up" means "You're such a slob."

The antidote to criticism is to make a complaint—to state our feelings and describe the situation neutrally, using words like "I'm *upset* that the *garbage hasn't been taken out*," instead of "You're too lazy to take out the garbage." Or, "I'm *disappointed* that *we couldn't have dinner together*," instead of "You're always late. Every time, you ruin our dinner together."

• **DEFENSIVENESS** is what we want to toss back when we feel criticized. When we perceive an attack, it's only natural to raise our arms to try to ward off our attacker. We can defend ourselves by (1) attacking back ("Well, so what if I'm late. You're a lousy cook"); (2) proclaiming our innocence ("I'm almost never late"); (3) being righteously indignant ("How dare you say I'm late—it's only three minutes past six"); or (4) whining like a victim ("I couldn't help it. My boss kept me late"). With phrases like these, we hide out and cover up that we have any responsibility for our problems. But in reality, the old adage "It takes two . . ." is true, and most of the time we're in there creating the problems we have, too.

So the antidote to defensiveness is to openly acknowledge our part in messing things up. It's as simple as saying, "Sorry, I am a few minutes late, aren't I?" But this is hard, too. We don't want to admit that we can do wrong. Unfortunately, most of us don't wear halos. We're human, and we make mistakes—better that we admit them and make peace than deny them and make war.

• **CONTEMPT** is our strongest predictor of divorce. When we're contemptuous, we sling criticism down on our partner from the pinnacle of our own superiority. Therefore, contempt is the epitome of disrespect. When we yell out insults, "graciously" give a condescending lecture, or call our partners bad names, we're being contemptuous. At its worst, contempt is verbal abuse. Verbal abuse destroys not only our relationships, but self-esteem and even the immune system of our partners. Examples range from pithy phrases like "You disgust me" to

"You asshole." Moderate contempt is a bit more subtle, like "How will you make it up to me for always being late?" Words like these destroy relationships, too—it just may take longer. But contempt doesn't have to involve words. There's also a cross-cultural facial expression of contempt that was discovered by researcher Dr. Paul Ekman. When we raise just the left corner of our mouth and create an unflattering dimple on the left side of our face, that's contempt. Also, if we roll our eyes, that's more contempt. In our research, we found that a husband's contempt predicts more frequent illness in his wife over the next four years. Contempt is toxic, indeed. What's the alternative? The antidote for contempt is to express our appreciation and respect for each other, to each other, in small ways, every day. How often do we say, "Thanks for doing the dishes," or "I love how you look when you're nursing Annie"? It's words like these that we need to say, often. They shouldn't stay bottled up inside us. Admiration and fondness, when they are outwardly expressed, go a long way toward creating a culture of appreciation in our homes—that's the antidote for contempt.

• STONEWALLING is the last of the Four Horsemen, and it means exactly what it sounds like. When we dislike what our partner is saying, we become like a stone wall and we give no response whatsoever. There are no "Uh-huhs," "I see's," or "Wows"—that is, our usual words of feedback. We don't move our face or even look at our partner, except to see whether the ogre has magically disappeared yet. In studying heterosexual relationships, we found that 85 percent of our stonewallers are men. Our studies also revealed that when people stonewall, their pulses are typically racing at over a hundred beats per minute ... while they're just sitting down and talking. That's physiologically very uncomfortable, like having the brake pedal and the accelerator floored at the same time. We reasoned that when we stonewall, we're attempting to eliminate all incoming stimuli (like our partner's voice) so that we can calm ourselves down. But the problem is that stonewalling drives our partners crazy. They feel shut out and want to reinvolve us. So they verbally or physically pursue us, which only overwhelms us more.

The antidote to stonewalling? If we get too overwhelmed, we need to take responsibility for our bodies' condition by taking a break, soothing ourselves, and making sure we come back to our partners within a reasonable time period. In this way, we can continue to talk to our partners more calmly in order to stay tuned in to them. Better yet, we can try to stay calm in the first place. Focusing on our breathing when we begin to get upset can be a big help. Finally, to counteract stonewalling, we can signal to our partners that we hear them, even if we only nod our heads or gaze into their eyes. These gestures reassure our partners that even if we don't agree, we're at least still there and wanting to listen.

With these Four Horsemen of the Apocalypse and their antidotes in mind, let's see how to bring up an issue using gentle start-up. The masters of the transition to parenthood follow three steps: First, they say what they feel. Second, they state what their feelings are about by describing the problem neutrally. And third, they express what they need. They can also be polite and sometimes appreciative. In sum, the three elements of gentle start-up are:

- *Say what you feel.*
- *Describe the problem neutrally, with no blame.*
- *Say what you need (not what you don't need).*

Here are some examples that compare a harsh start-up with a softened start-up.

HARSH START-UP: You don't care about me (blame). You only care about yourself (criticism). You are just wrapped up in your own little world, with your face stuck in that newspaper all the time (contempt and criticism).

SOFTENED START-UP: You know, right now I'm pretty upset (feeling) by your reading the newspaper at dinner and our not talking (neutral description of the problem). **Would you talk to me? Ask me how my day was, or tell me about yours, OK** (need)?

HARSH START-UP: **You think I'm ugly, don't you? You want someone skinny like the cover girls** (blame and implied criticism). **I know I'm heavy, but so what? I'm pregnant** (defensive at perceived attack—notice her partner hasn't said a word yet)!

SOFTENED START-UP: **I'm worried** (feeling) **that I'm not sexy enough for you now that I'm pregnant. We're going to this party, here I've put on this fancy dress, and it's too tight** (neutral description of the situation)! **I need some compliments from you. Now** (need)!

HARSH START-UP: **I'm sick and tired of you always taking your mother's side against me** (criticism). **Just a little momma's boy, aren't you** (contempt)?

SOFTENED START-UP: **I'm really mad** (feeling). **It seems like whenever your mom comes over I get left out** (neutral description of the problem). **Would you please pay attention to me and take my side if she gets critical tonight** (need)?

We can't do this perfectly every time. But we need to remember that communication is full of stumbling blocks. So if we aim for a gentle start-up to begin our conflict discussion, we're more likely to succeed in a conversation that ends with resolution or at least a compromise, not a stilted stalemate.

SELF-TEST ON START-UP

Are your arguments characterized by harsh start-up or gentle start-up? You and your partner can take the following self-test and see.

Read each statement and place a check mark in the appropriate TRUE (T) or FALSE (F) box.

WHEN WE DISCUSS OUR ISSUES:	YOU		YOUR PARTNER	
Arguments often seem to come out of nowhere.	T	F	T	F
I seem to always get blamed for them.	T	F	T	F
My partner criticizes my personality.	T	F	T	F
Our calm is suddenly shattered.	T	F	T	F
I find my partner's negativity unnerving and unsettling.	T	F	T	F

Did either of you answer "True" once, or more than once? If so, then your style of arguing is characterized by harsh start-up. You might find this next exercise especially useful.

Here's a great exercise for you to practice converting a harsh start-up into a softened start-up.

EXERCISE

SOFTENED START-UP

INSTRUCTIONS. Sit with your partner. Go through one item at a time. One of you reads aloud the first harsh start-up statement. Then the other partner thinks of a softened start-up that could be said instead, and says it. For item number two, you reverse roles. Keep going down the list, alternating roles. The partner who came up with the softened start-up last time becomes the reader for the next item, and vice versa. Remember, the three steps of a softened start-up are (1) I feel, (2) about what—a neutral description of the problem, and (3) I need. This needn't be a competition. Just have fun with it.

Examples

1. You think you're so cute! Stop flirting with other people.

Response: I'm feeling insecure about the party tonight. Would you stay with me through most of it?

Now you do it.

2. You're so rigid. Your views about religion are ridiculous.

3. You just want to work all the time and never be home with us.

4. You just don't care about the baby.

5. I'm so fat!

6. You never want sex anymore. You're like ice.

7. I am sick of all your emotional moods.

8. You just spend every dime I make. What about me?

9. Stop lying about your drugs!

10. She criticizes me all the time and you do nothing about it. You and your mother can go to hell.

11. I am sick of never going out. You never take me anywhere.

12. Stop criticizing my driving.

13. You never consult me. You always make all the decisions. You are so domineering!

14. You have no consideration about whether we get anywhere on time. That is so selfish.

15. How can I ever trust you? You never come home when you say you will. You're just in your own little world.

If you and your partner can master this exercise, it will be much easier to bring up your own problems. It may be hard at first. But just keep working on it, because the more you practice softened start-up, the smoother your conversations will get. Just like dancing.

5

ACCEPT INFLUENCE: THERE ARE TWO SIDES TO EVERY FIGHT

In a small village there was a famous rabbi who did marital counseling. This was the first day his new assistant, a young rabbi who was trying to learn therapy from the master, was with him, observing his every move. A couple, Mr. and Mrs. Goldstein, sat in the rabbi's waiting room. The rabbi first called in Mrs. Goldstein, and introduced his assistant. "What seems to be the problem?" the rabbi asked her. She proceeded to complain bitterly about her marriage. He's horrible in this way, and he's horrible in that way, she said. After twenty minutes, the rabbi stopped her. He said, "Mrs. Goldstein, I have now heard you complain for twenty minutes, and I have to tell you that you are completely right. I think it is unbelievable what you have to put up with, with that man, and still you keep giving and giving to your family. I have tremendous admiration for you." Mrs. Goldstein then said, "Oh, Rabbi, it feels so good that someone finally understands me. Thank you." And she left. The rabbi next called in Mr. Goldstein. "What seems to be the problem?" the rabbi asked him. He also proceeded to complain bitterly about his wife. After twenty minutes, the rabbi stopped him and said, "Mr. Goldstein, I have now heard you complain for twenty minutes, and I have to tell you that you are completely right. I think it is unbelievable what you have to tolerate with that woman, and still you keep giving and giving to your family. I have tremendous admiration for

65

you." Mr. Goldstein then said, "Oh, Rabbi, it feels so good that someone finally understands me. Thank you." And he left. The assistant then turned to the rabbi and said, "Rabbi, you said that Mrs. Goldstein was right." "Yes," said the rabbi. "Rabbi, you also said that Mr. Goldstein was right." "Yes," said the rabbi. "They can't *both* be right!" said the assistant. "You know, you're absolutely right," said the rabbi.

Our point is that in any argument or miscommunication, there is not one objective, absolute reality. There are always two subjective realities, both of them right in their own way. Our conflict discussions backfire when we insist that our perception is the only one that's right, which, of course, makes our partner's perception wrong. We convert our arguments into wrestling matches in which one of us wins, and the other one loses. In the end, we both lose. Couples tend to see their job in a dispute as persuading their partner of their position, instead of understanding their partner's position. Just imagine instead what would happen if *both* people viewed it as their first job in a dispute to understand their *partner's* position instead of arguing for their own position.

Because, in a dispute, we both feel that we are objectively right and our partner is objectively wrong, we've heard many partners exclaim, "If I just had a videotape of that last conversation, you would see how wrong you are." But in our lab, we do film couples having arguments, and when we play back the tapes for our couples, they still come up with two different views of what happened. Both partners had their own point of view, and both thought that they were objectively right.

Imagine that you've been asked to paint a picture of a potted purple plant on a stand. You sit directly in front of the plant and paint it. Your partner sits off to the side and paints it, too. Will your pictures be identical? Not likely. Our conflicts are like potted plants. We each have our own perspective on them. The light on the stems, the colors of the leaves, the shadows on the stand, and the angles and forms all differ, depending on where we sit. Yet it is as if we try to convince each other that our picture is the only true picture that's real.

Let's imagine that we've just had an argument. Our partner forgot to pick up the tickets for a concert we're supposed to attend tonight. We're mad at him and we say so, but with harsh start-up. He yells back in self-defense, then retreats to another room. We both wind up nursing hurt feelings. Neither one of us is blameless, but when later we review what just happened, we both see ourselves as the victim of our partner's actions and mostly innocent of any wrongdoing. It is very human to be much more forgiving of ourselves than our partners. Psychologist Fritz Heider called this "the fundamental attribution error." Translated, it means that it's human nature to think, "I'm OK; you're defective," and it leads to "I'm right; you're wrong."

When we're like the disasters in the transition to parenthood, we set about to prove how right we are. As our partner is talking, we are listening with only half our mind, formulating our rebuttal with the other half. We immediately respond with rebuttal when it's our turn to talk. We haven't fully listened, but we assume that persuasion will work an amazing miracle. Our partner's rebuttal of our rebuttal makes us defensive, and as we become defensive we tend to repeat ourselves. We call it the "summarizing yourself syndrome." Somehow even during the thirty-second time we explain our point of view, we picture that when our partner hears us this time she will suddenly slap her forehead and say, "Oh, now I get it. What was I thinking? Now I can see that you are right and I was wrong. I feel so close to you now. Let's make love." But that's not ever going to happen.

Social psychologist Anatol Rapoport became a leading expert in international conflict. He wrote about fights, games, debates, diplomatic battles, violence, the cold war, and hot wars between countries. He was most interested in disputes he called "debates" in international conflicts in which it was possible for persuasion to influence someone else's point of view. We have applied his ideas to couples.

His secret about reducing threat in these debates and disputes was very simple:

Postpone persuasion

He suggested that neither party in a dispute be able to persuade the other party they were right until they could state the opposition's point of view to their satisfaction. So each party's job was to first *ask questions* in order to understand the other party's point of view, and then to *restate it*. Of course, the other party's viewpoint initially made no sense. But when more questions were asked, the clouds gradually cleared. There was more understanding. Rapoport found that when both parties delayed persuasion until after there was understanding, both sides became more reasonable and less defensive. Also, they both felt more respected. So instead of being adversaries, they often became allies, working together on a mutual problem. Understanding and feeling understood lubricated the processes of persuasion.

Rapoport had discovered a secret about disputes: We need to be able to state our version of our partner's point of view to *our partner's satisfaction* before stating our own point of view. To accomplish this, we need to ask our partner open-ended questions. Open-ended questions are questions that yield more than a one-word answer like yes or no. Answers to them are more complex and take more thought. They differ from close-ended questions, which are more like "Are you going to the grocery store?" (Yes or no.) An open-ended question is more like an invitation, whereas an immediate rebuttal is more like a rejection. So, during a conflict, instead of saying, "Here. Take this rebuttal!" and being met with "Oh, yeah? Take that rebuttal!" we need to ask an open-ended question, like "What makes that so important to you?" or "Can you help me to understand this better?"

We also need to be able to make what Rapoport called "the assumption of similarity." What he meant by that was what one of our clients called "giving our partner the benefit of the doubt." Rapoport said that we need to assume that our partner doesn't possess all the negative traits in this discussion, nor that we possess all the positive traits. Rapoport suggested that if we find ourselves attributing a negative quality to only our partner, we should try to also see some of this same negative quality in ourselves. Furthermore, if we attribute a positive quality only to ourselves, we should try to also see some of this same positive quality in our partner. Imagine in a dispute if we first thought, "The nerve of my partner to be so angry at me," and then thought, "Well, what do you know, I guess I am also angry here! We're both angry." Imagine if we first thought, "I am the only one being rational here," and then thought, "Well, actually, I know that my partner is also a very rational person with a lot of common sense. I guess we can both talk about this problem logically." These ideas of assuming that we are similar (negatively and positively) are so simple. Yet they counter the all-too-human tendency to think, "I'm OK; you're defective."

Let's watch a couple who are arguing about money. He wants to spend more on having fun, and she wants to save more for the future. Instead of just loudly repeating themselves, imagine how good it would sound if they talked like this.

> HE: Can I ask you a question? Let me see if I understand you. Do you think we're not saving enough money, and you're scared about the future? Is that it?
>
> **She:** Right . . . (*A while later*) For you, are you feeling sort of trapped, like we can't have any fun because I'm holding on to the purse strings too tightly?

At this point, no one is doing any persuasion. Instead, they're each attempting to paraphrase what they've heard their partners say, then checking it out with a question to make sure they've got it right.

Here's a list of useful open-ended questions to keep handy for your conflict discussions.

- *What do you feel about this?*
- *What do you think about this?*
- *What makes this so important to you?*
- *What's the worst part about this for you?*
- *Is there something you're afraid of here, and if so, what is it?*
- *What is it that you value here?*

Now, there's one more step before persuasion can begin: We also need to *validate* our partner's point of view. Essentially, this means acknowledging that our partners have a right to feel the way they do. In short, we need to say that their viewpoint makes sense to us, even if it's different from our own. We haven't lost our own reality; we're just stepping into our partner's shoes for a moment. It's as simple as saying, "I get it," or "Good point." This helps our partners feel understood . . . and respected. If you have trouble with this, try completing the sentence "Your views make sense to me because . . ." Validating involves not just knowing what our partner is feeling, or feeling some of what our partner is feeling, but being able to see the world (on this issue) from our partner's eyes, to see why it makes some sense to have those feelings. Communicating all this is real validation.

Combining these concepts together—acknowledging that there are two sides to every fight, restating our partner's point of view to our partner's satisfaction, and validating our partner's point of view— yields one of the most important ingredients in managing conflict: *accepting influence from our partner.* When we accept our partner's influence during a discussion, we are honoring our partner as someone who is intelligent, thoughtful, and well intentioned. Who can resist feeling so respected? Accepting influence is a great aphrodisiac.

Here's a self-test to see how your relationship measures up on accepting influence.

Read each statement and place a check mark in the appropriate TRUE or FALSE box.

WHEN WE DISCUSS OUR ISSUES ...	YOU		YOUR PARTNER	
I generally want my partner to feel influential in this relationship.	T	F	T	F
I can listen to my partner make his or her point.	T	F	T	F
My partner has a lot of basic common sense.	T	F	T	F
I don't reject my partner's opinions out of hand.	T	F	T	F
My partner is basically a great help as a problem solver.	T	F	T	F

If you and your partner answered "True" to all of these items, then your relationship is doing fine on accepting influence. If you didn't, then your relationship probably needs some work in this area.

Here's an exercise.

EXERCISE

RAPOPORT METHOD

INSTRUCTIONS. Have two notepads and two pencils handy. From the items on the list that follows, decide on one issue (and only one) that the two of you will discuss. Keep in mind that you're only selecting a topic to give yourselves something to discuss so you can practice your new skills. Any topic will do. Put a check mark next to it, then describe it in more detail on the form below the list. Then each of you take turns being the speaker or the listener.

Here's a formula for the speaker. The speaker will state his or her own point of view for no more than ten minutes. Set a timer if necessary. To make this as constructive as possible, the speaker can talk about what he or she needs (not what he or she does not need). That could mean transforming a complaint into your own longing and into your need. Then ask for what you need, and explain why this need is so important to you.

The listener will ask open-ended questions to understand the speaker's point of view and also take notes on it in writing. As you listen, make sure to counter the tendency to think, "I'm okay; you're defective," with the assumption of similarity. Then the listener will summarize the speaker's point of view, and validate it. Now switch roles. The listener will become the speaker, and the speaker will become the listener, and you'll repeat the same process again with the roles reversed. Be sure not to argue for your point of view. Instead, postpone persuasion, and work to deepen the understanding between you.

Things We Disagree About (Check Only One for This Exercise)

- Time with baby versus work
- What we eat
- Punctuality
- Neatness
- Our friends
- Dividing up the housework fairly: who does what
- The role of in-laws or relatives
- Drugs and alcohol
- Jealousy
- Our personal goals
- Religion
- Having fun
- Talking to each other about stress
- Balancing work and family
- Affection
- Sex, romance, or affection

■ Money

■ Recreation or exercise

OUR TOPIC IS:

WHAT I FEEL AND NEED:

MY PARTNER'S POINT OF VIEW (What my partner feels and needs):

MY PARTNER'S POINT OF VIEW MAKES SENSE TO ME BECAUSE:
(Tell your partner that.)

6

CALM DOWN BY SELF-SOOTHING

Marie and Ruben drive their black Mustang down the highway, doing eighty-five miles per hour. We've mounted a tiny videotape camera in their car. They also wear finger devices we've given them to monitor their heart rates. They are red-faced and yelling. Let's listen in . . .

RUBEN: Teresa is not my wife anymore. You're my wife. She's my ex-wife. This is all about my daughter, my Melanie. Teresa's going to take us back to court if I make her mad. She wants Melanie back. Don't you get that?

MARIE: Stop yelling at me. I don't see why you have to be such a chump with Teresa. You're like putty in her hands. Where's your backbone?

RUBEN: Leave me alone! I'm not going to lose Melanie just because you think I should be nasty to her mother. Forget it.

MARIE: But she's calling me bad names behind my back. And every time you go to pick up Melanie, her hands are all over you.

RUBEN: So what? I'm not touching her. I can't control what she does. And some wife you turned out to be. You don't get within fifty yards of me. Since Robbie was born, you're the big ice woman.

MARIE: Is that all you think about? You disgust me. That baby is all that keeps me around here.

RUBEN: And it's a miracle I stick around at all. Teresa would welcome me back with open arms.

As they fight, his heartbeat races at 135 beats a minute, and hers at 140. They'd rather be on Pluto than in this car together at this moment. They throw words into the air, and no one listens. Alone in their misery, they each hope that some miracle will occur and their partner will magically be replaced by a compassionate saint. So many different issues are being tossed back and forth like Ping-Pong balls in the car, but which ones are *really* being discussed? It's impossible to tell. We don't have a linear conversation here. All we've got is chaos. Why did they end up fighting like this? Why does anyone fight like this?

Over thirty years ago, John began a research collaboration with Professor Robert Levenson (who was the best man at our wedding, incidentally). Robert and John decided to study what happens inside the bodies of two people when they have a conflict conversation with one another. They asked couples to sit in chairs facing one another and to discuss a problem for fifteen minutes. While the couples talked, they videotaped them. They also measured their heart rates, blood velocities to the finger and ear, how much their palms sweated, and how much they jiggled around in their chairs. What they discovered was shocking. Some partners' heart rates ran as high as 168 beats a minute while just sitting and talking!

Three years later they recontacted the couples. They discovered that some relationships had deteriorated over that time, while others stayed level or rose higher in happiness. But then, while looking at the physiology of their subjects during the initial problem discussions, here's what they found.

The people whose relationships had deteriorated were the very ones whose heart rates had shot up sky high three years ago. They had also had racing blood velocity and sweatier palms—all indicating high physiological arousal. Robert and John had thought they might find *some* linkage between relationship decline and heightened physiology, but these bodily factors proved uncannily accurate at foretelling the future.

What was going on here? From the internal body readings they'd obtained in these partners, Robert and John realized that during conflict discussions, some partners' bodies were firing off as if they were in mortal danger. Physiologically, they looked like they were trying to avoid Attila the Hun. Their reactions weren't a conscious choice, either. The partners would simply be sitting and talking, but then subconsciously they'd perceive that their partners were attacking them. Then the alarm bells would go off deep inside their brains, outside their awareness, shattering their internal state of well-being. In a split second, lower brain centers would take over the controls.

John and Robert were seeing a "general-alarm" response that has evolved in our species over millions of years. Here's how it works: When we see danger, a cascade of events floods our body. First, the longest nerve in our body, the vagus nerve, takes the brakes off our heart. Our heart immediately speeds up. If it jacks up over a hundred beats a minute (or eighty beats a minute if we're athletic), our body starts secreting adrenaline. Now our heart says, "Get that blood out there," and contracts harder as well as racing faster.

But at the same time, our general-alarm system also dreads an attack that might cause hemorrhaging. So our blood flow changes course. Blood flow shuts down to our gut and kidneys. Blood from the periphery of our arms and legs gets shuffled off to our central core, and our kidneys heighten blood pressure and conserve fluid volume—all to minimize the damage of potential wounds.

Other parts of our body get busy, too. Our adrenal glands stimulate the secretion of adrenaline and a stress hormone called cortisol, and our liver converts glycogen into glucose and releases it into our bloodstream so sugar can fuel our blood. Meanwhile, blood keeps pumping hard to our brain to keep us alert.

We call this tidal wave of physiological events *diffuse physiological arousal*, or DPA. The generic term for it is "fight or flight." What's most astounding is that we are rarely aware of it while it's happening. It's like sitting and reading the paper, then being stunned when we suddenly find ourselves floating in three feet of water. Most of us are terrible at guessing what our heart rates are. We think we're calm and steady when we're actually drowning.

DPA also divides the genders. Robert Levenson and his graduate student Loren Carter compared men and women in DPA. With their consent, men and women experienced a sound like a gunshot that triggered a startle response. The heart rates of men took off like a jackrabbit's, while the rates for women were more like a slow gallop. Then the men took much longer than women to calm down. When Carter and Levenson queried their people about their emotions after being startled, women reported fear, while men answered anger and contempt. Did the men need revenge before they could settle down?

Evolution has probably fostered these differences between men and women. Anthropologists tell us that as far back as they know, a man served to protect the tribe and to hunt cooperatively for large game. So, to survive, he'd hear a sound and race off with his tribemates, ready to ambush the invader, while his mate would wait like a deer in the thicket, calm and still nursing her young. Groups of men hunted together cooperatively. The distances between them were long, so they had to silently signal to each other, staying quiet so as not to frighten off their prey. They had to remain vigilant in the face of danger.

Meanwhile, in times of peace, the women collectively gathered roots, nuts, and berries or trapped small animals, often as they nursed their babies. We can imagine them chatting amicably as they moved quietly through the bushes together. Now, breast milk can't be released in anything but a calm body. The hormone oxytocin works like magic to trigger the milk letdown response, but is only secreted when a woman is internally as quiet as a still night. Oxytocin has other nurturant properties, too—it promotes affiliation and social bonding. So women formed better bonds with other women than men did with other men.

Ten thousand years later, where does that leave us? Full of good survivors: men with their quiet vigilance and hyperalertness (as if they are still watching out for invaders), and women with their warmth and affiliative strengths. Put these together in a lab with a good argument at hand, and what do we get? The male hyperalertness and genetic propensity for remaining silent is paired with the female need to stay calm and face issues by connecting so that the couple can bond better. No wonder we human couples run into so much trouble during conflict.

The problem of DPA grows even more complex when we look at how it alters our perceptions and behavior here and now. When we're in DPA, our peripheral vision is diminished, and our hearing is compromised. Surges of adrenaline give us "tunnel vision." So we see danger lurking everywhere, even when it's not there. That's what DPA can do.

The case of Amadou Diallo sadly illustrates this phenomenon. Shift to a scary neighborhood in New York in the late 1990s, patrolled by four rookie cops. In a series of rapidly escalating misjudgments, in just eight seconds a dark man in a doorway was dead with nineteen bullets in him. When they yelled, "Freeze," and he mistakenly reached for his wallet to get out his ID, they figured he was going for something else. One of the rookies yelled out, "Gun!" They all fired at once. Diallo died instantly. But there was no gun. He was pulling out his identification from a black wallet. He didn't understand English well enough to comply with their orders. Probably in an escalated state of DPA, they had not taken the time to find out that he was a recent immigrant who lived there. In their DPA, the wallet was mistaken for a gun. The rookies probably hadn't been on the job long enough to have learned how to stay calm. Their fear may have facilitated the tragic and deadly error in perception. In other deadly force encounters, police must deal with similar situations in which the danger is quite real.

Most of us don't routinely face danger in our work. But it can feel that way at home when we fight with our partners. Our bodies are geared to respond to danger. Behind our familiar faces, we sometimes respond as if the terrors were real. The result is that during our bad arguments, we can become distressed and go into DPA, just like the rookie cops. We can be talking about something as benign as who will do the laundry when some ancient trigger will fire and we're off and running. If we don't learn how to deal with our DPA, it can diminish our relationships, too, as it did with the couples in John's lab.

A not-so-trivial side note is that when we go into DPA chronically over and over again during our arguments, our bodies become worn down. Chronic DPA can suppress the functioning of our immune system and contribute to our physical deterioration. As proof, for over three decades psychologists have witnessed the correlation between hostile or disintegrating relationships and lots of illnesses, including cancer and heart disease. Recent research has directly linked couples' conflict with immunosuppression.

We inherited the general-alarm response from our ancestors, who needed it to mobilize for action. Those were times when there were many predators and humanity was the unprotected prey. But times have changed. We don't have to fear leopards in the trees anymore. For most of us, thankfully, our partners are not our predators. Yet, during disagreements or hurt feelings with our partners, conflict can still evoke that instinctive DPA response. DPA affects our ability to take in information. We become very poor listeners. We are not able to problem solve, be compassionate, or be creative. In DPA, our physiologies put us into a protective mode that does not process information very well. As we try to listen, we simultaneously form our rebuttal. So we listen with only half our mind. We tend to become defensive, and we tend to repeat ourselves in what we call the "summarizing yourself syndrome." We hardly ever summarize and validate what our partner is saying, or summarize the common points of both.

The way to start conquering the effects of DPA is through awareness. We must learn to recognize the subtle signs of it building early on before it enflames and engulfs us. When it's just a flicker in the gut and a change in breathing (quickening or holding the breath), we can learn to quiet it down and soothe ourselves. Then we can stay in the here and now with our mates and actually discuss our problems calmly, and not run from or strike out at the predator like our prehistoric noble ancestors of the bush.

A first step in building awareness is to take a self-test. Let's see whether your relationship is troubled by DPA. The following self-test will ask you questions about "flooding." Flooding is the psychological state related to DPA. If you find that you get "flooded" during discussions with your partner, it's likely that DPA is troubling your relationship.

SELF-TEST ON FLOODING

Read each statement and place a check mark in the appropriate TRUE or FALSE box.

WHEN WE DISCUSS OUR PROBLEMS . . .	YOU		YOUR PARTNER	
	T	F	T	F
Our discussions get too heated.	□	□	□	□
I have a hard time calming down.	□	□	□	□
One of us is going to say something we will regret.	□	□	□	□
I think to myself, "Why can't we talk more logically?"	□	□	□	□
My partner has a long list of unreasonable demands.	□	□	□	□

If either of you answered "True" to one or more of the items above, the chances are that you get flooded during your conflicts and are in DPA at those times.

LONELINESS

There's one more sign for us that DPA may be an unwelcome visitor in our home. This one often shows up at our door a few months after our babies arrive. When we're worn out and tired and we've had lots of fights with escalations into DPA, we begin to avoid each other in order to keep things quiet around our baby, and calmer for ourselves. So we don't face those nasty problems that keep surfacing. Instead, we dive deep like a mole underground and bury inside us our needs to be heard, to be respected, and to find resolution. This process of avoidance is subtle; we don't realize it's happening. We just work more at our jobs, or call Mom more, or talk to our friends but not our partners. We start living our lives in parallel, running alongside each other, like two railroad tracks, coming together hardly ever. Perhaps our lives are a bit calmer avoiding conflict, but eventually avoidance plays its hand, and one day we find ourselves waking up feeling empty, lonely, and hopeless. Then the baby cries and needs feeding, and we're off on our day—one of us steps away into the kitchen, while the other leaves for work—with still no connection between us.

Is this happening in your relationship? If so, DPA may be the culprit, and learning to calm it down and tame it may be the solution. Take this next self-test with your partner to find out more.

SELF-TEST ON EMOTIONAL WITHDRAWAL AND LONELINESS

Read each statement and place a check mark in the appropriate TRUE or FALSE box.

STATEMENT	YOU		YOUR PARTNER	
I often find myself disappointed in this relationship.	T	F	T	F
I will at times find myself quite lonely in this relationship.	T	F	T	F
It is hard for my deepest feelings to get much attention in this relationship.	T	F	T	F
There is not enough closeness between us.	T	F	T	F
I have adapted to a lot in this relationship and I am not so sure it's a good idea.	T	F	T	F

If either of you answered "True" to one or more of the items above, the chances are that loneliness and emotional withdrawal are playing a role in your relationship, and you need help with reducing loneliness.

THE SOLUTION TO DPA: TAKE BREAKS AND SELF-SOOTHE

We discovered the power of taking a break one day during a pilot study in our lab. We were researching what would happen to heart rates in couples after they'd argued, escalated, and flown into DPA, and we decided to do a little experiment. We told each of our couples, fictitiously, that our equipment had broken down and they'd need to wait a bit before continuing their discussion. We asked them to please stop talking until the equipment was repaired, and we kindly provided them with various magazines to read. We were actually monitoring their heart rates. After their heart rates resumed a normal pace, we declared the equipment all fixed, and asked them to resume their conversation.

Lo and behold, in most cases, the conversations changed completely. For many couples, it was as if they'd just had a brain transplant. The warriors had stepped out of the room and the peacemakers had returned. The couples had become much more reasonable, flexible, collaborative, and even kind with one another. We'd stumbled onto a secret. The only thing required was for a couple to take a break, just long enough to get those heart rates down. Then the partners could discuss a problem with equanimity—and without DPA wreaking havoc.

Remember Marie and Ruben arguing as they sped down the highway at breakneck speed, with their heart rates soaring? We saw Marie and Ruben in therapy later, in our relationship clinic. It turns out that they were having lots of escalating quarrels, especially after their new baby arrived. There were problems with Ruben's ex-wife and Marie's jealousy, and the ex-wife making hell out of Ruben's visits with his oldest daughter. Moreover, Marie and Ruben hadn't had sex since the baby was born. DPA was running rampant everywhere, and Marie and Ruben were growing more distant and lonely by the minute.

In therapy, we equipped both of them with inexpensive portable wristwatch heart-rate monitors. We use them so often now that we now sell them on our website (www.gottman.com). We set the monitors so that a beeper would sound if their heart rates rose above a hundred beats per minute, and we asked them to put on the monitors before discussing any issue. If the beeper went off, that was their signal to stop talking, take a break, and do some self-soothing alone before returning to their partners and finishing the discussion. We taught them the steps of self-soothing. They did just as we instructed. We also worked on methods to improve their conflict discussions—the same methods you're learning.

The intervention was a balm to their battles. Soon they were fighting less, calmly reaching more compromises, and DPA was rarely a problem. Their discussions could still be emotional, just not escalated by the Four Horsemen. Their discussions became more productive, they grew closer and happier, and their romantic life sparked with new passion. After our intervention, we have followed this couple for ten years. Their relationship improvements lasted. There were no more dangerous screaming matches down the highway.

HOW AND WHEN TO TAKE A BREAK

We know we need to take a break when we begin to feel flooded. Some of us may feel a knot in our stomachs, or our jaws tightening, or our breathing going shallow. Our arms or legs may begin to twitch. Or we may freeze up and be utterly unable to move. We may think our partner's eyes are lasers that will burn us if we look into them. We may get sudden images in our heads of dashing out the door, or yelling at our partner to shut up, or even slapping our partner. Angry and hurtful words may spring into our heads. One of our research subjects advised, "You've got to stop long before you get there. When I notice that she keeps talking and I'm not feeling any calmer, and things aren't going the way I want them to go, I know I'm reaching my boiling point and it's time to take a break."

During a conversation, if any of these signs of flooding and DPA show up, it's time to ask for a break. It will help our partner to stop if we tell them how long the break will last and when we intend to come back and resume talking. Make an actual time to come back together again and talk—and not in the year 2043. A break should last at least half an hour, and at most a day. Otherwise, it may feel like passive-aggressive punishment. And at least half an hour is necessary because it takes that long for the chemicals released during DPA to diffuse through our interstitial tissues, get picked up by our capillaries, and travel to our kidneys and down into our bladder, where they no longer act on the body. Then they can't affect us any longer.

Sometimes it's tough to find time in our busy schedule to get back to a conflict discussion, especially when we want to avoid it.

What with kids, jobs, and home life, finding time the same day may seem impossible. But that's the goal. If the interim time stretches out beyond a day, it's helpful to schedule a date and time when the discussion can continue. As long as we know that it will continue, the partner who wasn't in DPA is usually willing to wait.

Another important component of taking a break is our thinking during the break. We may take a walk around the block, play or listen to music, or soak in a hot bath—whatever comforts us. But if we are muttering to ourselves, "I don't have to take this. Nobody talks to me that way. I'm going to show my partner a thing or two," we might as well be back in the boxing ring for all the good it will do. Our righteous indignation is perpetuating our DPA. Or if we're playing the victim, we're sighing, "Why is my partner always picking on me? What about all the sacrifices I've made for this relationship? And never do I get a word of gratitude. I'm never going to open my mouth again." This innocent-victim role usually leads people to want to whine. And there's no good vintage of this whine. All the years of that vineyard are sour. Worse, we're still maintaining our DPA.

The best thoughts for us are self-soothing ones. The ideal is to remember that our partner is basically a good person, and so are we. We do not have the corner on all the positive human traits, nor does our partner have the corner on all the negative human traits. Our partner can figure out what they're responsible for in this conflict; we don't need to do it for them. We do need to sort out our part in it. That means focusing on what we've said or done that has contributed to the fight. It also helps to think about what we do need from our partner, not what we don't need. For example, it won't work to come back and say, "Dear, I need you to never speak in that tone to me again." We'll sound condescending and critical. But we can say, "Dear, I need you to speak to me gently and quietly. That works best for me." We have a much better chance of being heard with "dos" rather than "don'ts."

The final ingredient of a good break is how we physically soothe ourselves. There are hundreds of methods to use. Some of us may walk around the block, talk to someone, watch TV, or read a book. Others may pet the dog, hold the cat, or scrub the floor. Still others may practice yoga, do some meditation, or play the piano. Anything can work as long as it is personally comforting to us.

One of the best methods of self-soothing that we've found combines deep muscle relaxation with guided imagery. Five steps are involved: breathing evenly and deeply; tensing and then relaxing muscle groups; sensing heaviness in the muscles; feeling warmth in the muscles; and, finally, envisioning being in a special place of tranquillity and peace.

We've provided two exercises below to help you take a break that can soothe you. These exercises should be done whenever your conflict discussion is heating up to boiling.

EXERCISE

FLOODING—DEVELOP A BREAK RITUAL

INSTRUCTIONS. The two of you need to agree on a signal you will use when one of you is flooded. Lots of people agree to use the time-out signal of football referees, or others, a hand held up to indicate "stop." Whichever one you choose, make sure you both agree to it. When either one of you uses it, the other person needs to reply with words like "OK, you're flooded. Let's stop and take a break. See you in thirty minutes, all right?" That way, you'll have an understanding that regardless of when or why, the break signal will be respected and followed. Take a few minutes to discuss each of the following questions.

- What nonverbal signal should we use for indicating we need to take a break (no rude gestures, please)?
- Can we commit to giving each other a break when the signal is given? Even if one of us is flooded while the other one is not?

▨ How should we handle setting a time to return and continue to talk? For example, should it be a given amount of time, like thirty minutes for every break, or should we decide at that moment how long we need?

Once you've decided on the details of your break ritual, proceed to the next exercise.

EXERCISE

SELF-SOOTHING

INSTRUCTIONS. This is an exercise that you can do separately or together. It works nicely if one of you reads to your partner aloud the directions that follow that will direct your partner to self-soothe. So, one of you reads the directions, while the other one listens and follows them. Or make a tape of your partner's voice. Then you can trade roles, so both of you get a chance to experience this relaxation. If you wish to make this a solitary exercise, we suggest you read the directions aloud into a tape recorder, then play it back for yourself to hear and to follow. Make sure that whoever reads uses a quiet and calm voice tone.

You will be directed to do five steps.

▨ Breathe deeply and evenly, from the diaphragm.

▨ Tense one muscle group at a time, holding the tension, then relaxing it.

▨ Sense your muscles as heavy.

▨ Feel warmth in your muscles.

▨ Envision a soothing image of tranquillity and peace.

Try taking your heart rate just before and just after you do this exercise.

Directions for Self-Soothing.

Find a position that is comfortable. Now sit back or lie down and try to get comfortable. Comfortable? OK.

We will start with deep breathing. Place your hand on your stomach.

Breathe in deeply and evenly. You should feel your stomach push out as you inhale. Now, exhale slowly and evenly. You should feel your stomach drop back down again. Make sure your belly moves out and away from your backbone when you inhale, and back when you exhale. That's it. Good. Again, inhale and push your belly out. Now exhale, and drop your belly down. Inhale . . . exhale . . . that's it. Got it? OK. Now continue to breathe with a count of 1-2 when you inhale, and 1-2-3-4 when you exhale. Keep your breathing slow and even and natural. An ideal relaxation rate is about six to ten breaths a minute. In just this way, take five more breaths.

Very good.

Just let your mind drift, as if you were on a cloud, floating very lazily and very relaxed through the air, your mind drifting. Now let's begin.

Let's start with your legs. Lift your left leg straight in front of you. Pull your toe up toward your knee and tense all the muscles in your leg, your thigh muscles, your calf muscles, your entire leg. Hold that tension (for the count of 4). Now drop your leg back down. Lift your right leg straight in front of you. Pull your toe up toward your knee and tense all the muscles in your right leg, your thigh muscles, your calf muscles, your entire leg. Hold that tension (for the count of 4). Now drop your leg back down. Let all the tension flow out of your legs as if it was a liquid flowing out of your legs and down into the earth. Let it all out, let it all flow out. Take a deep breath in and let it out, slowly and evenly. Feel the floor (or the chair) pressing up on your legs, feel them getting heavy, as if they are becoming like lead weights, feel them heavy now, very heavy. Now they are getting this warm, heavy feeling, getting very warm. Both arms and hands and legs are getting heavy and warm.

Let your mind drift, on a cloud, floating and very relaxed, drifting.

Let's move on to your back. Tense your back by arching your back way up high and pulling your shoulders back. Feel all that tension in your lower back. We hold ourselves up there. Now hold the tension (count to 4), and now let it go, let go of the tension, let all the tension flow out of your back, down your legs, through your feet, and down into the floor. Let it all out, let it all flow out. Take a deep breath in, and slowly let it out. Take another deep breath in and let it out, slowly, evenly. Beautiful. Feel the floor (or the chair) supporting your whole body. Feel your whole back getting heavy, heavy, and now getting a warm feeling, like lying on a warm blanket.

Now let's move on to your abdomen and middle back. Tense your stomach and abdomen muscles by pulling in your stomach really tight. Now hold this tension (count to 4), and let it go, let go of the tension, let your belly completely relax. Take a deep breath in and let it out, slowly and evenly. Take another deep breath in . . . and out again. Let your belly feel heavy, warm and heavy, as if you've just swallowed some warm milk.

Let your mind just drift, on a cloud, floating and very relaxed, drifting.

Now let's start with your arms. Raise your arms straight in front of you and reach for the opposite wall (or ceiling). Clench your fists, hard . . . now straighten your fingers and stretch them. Here's where we hold anger. Tense those arms and hold the tension (count to 4), and now let it go and drop your arms back down again. Let go of the tension, let all the tension flow out as if it were a liquid flowing out of your arms, down into the earth. Take a deep breath in, and let it out, slowly and evenly.

Feel the floor (or the chair) pressing against your arms, feel your arms getting heavy, as if they are becoming like lead weights, feel them heavy now, very heavy. Now they are getting this warm, heavy feeling, getting very warm. Concentrate on getting this feeling of warmth and heaviness in your arms. Take a deep breath in and let it out, slowly and evenly.

Let your mind drift for a moment, on a cloud, floating and very relaxed, drifting.

Let's move up to your shoulders. Raise your shoulders up toward your ears, as high as you can get them. Higher . . . That's where all that responsibility is. Now hold it (count to 4), and now let it go, let go of the tension, let all that responsibility flow down from your shoulders, down through your arms, down through your legs and feet, and down into the earth. Feel the floor (or the chair) supporting you completely, feel your neck and shoulders getting very relaxed and warm. Arms and hands and legs and belly and back and neck and shoulders are getting very heavy and warm. Take a deep breath in and let it out, slowly and evenly. Take another deep breath in and let it out, slowly and evenly.

Let your mind drift, on a cloud, floating and very relaxed, drifting, getting very relaxed now. Take a deep breath in and let it out, slowly and evenly. Take another deep breath in and let it out, slowly and evenly.

Let's move on to your face. Clench your jaws tightly together. Here's where we hold all our frustration. Hold that tension (count to 4), and now let it go. Slowly circle your lower jaw first in one direction, and now reverse the direction. And now raise your eyebrows up toward the top of your forehead. Now hold that tension (count to 4), and now let it go, let go of the tension, let all the tension flow out. Now squeeze your eyes tightly closed—here's how we say "No." Block out all the negativity of the world as you shut your eyes. Now hold that tension (count to 4), and now let it go, let go of the tension, let all the tension flow. Take a deep breath in and let it out, nice and slow.

Now imagine yourself standing beneath a nice warm waterfall. Feel the water washing away every last ounce of tension from your body—warm blue water washing away your stress, your tension. All the tension is flowing down with the water, down into the ground, from your head down over your shoulders, down over your arms, down your hands, down the trunk of your body, down your legs, down your feet, and down into the ground. You're completely relaxed now. Just enjoy this lovely shower.

Now is your moment to take yourself to your own private sanctuary, a beautiful place that's there just for you. A place that is quiet where you can feel peaceful, still, in harmony with all around you. It is a reassuring place, a soothing place. It might be a sandy beach, or a mountaintop, or a warm waterfall, or a cool pine forest, or a comforting room. It might be cool and raining softly there, or it might be sunny and warm. Imagine every detail of this place. See the colors there, the shapes there, the forms, the shadows. See if you can hear anything. See if you can smell anything. Feel how the air touches your skin. What does it feel like? Enjoy this place. Take a few minutes to just savor it, for this is your own very special place, your own personal and private retreat. You can take yourself there anytime you want to. All you have to do is to see it in your mind's eye and you'll be there. It will always be there inside of you. Now, take a deep breath in and let it out, slowly and evenly. And when you're ready, bring yourself back to this room, and when you're ready, open your eyes. Hello.

7

COMPROMISE

Now that we're good and relaxed and the problem is on the table, what next? It's time to compromise. Nobody wins or loses in compromise. We gain a little of what we want, and surrender a little, too.

A group of eight-year-old boys and girls nicely illustrated this point for us. Eight-year-olds are very logical. Here's what we said: "We are therapists. We help mommies and daddies to solve some of their problems about fighting with each other. We'd like to ask you for your advice."

"OK." They thought our request was totally natural.

"We have one couple who are always fighting about money. He thinks she spends too much money, and he gets mad at her. She wants to enjoy life, spend money, and not just live for the future. So she likes to spend money. And she also gets mad at him. What should they do?" Without hesitation, a little hand shot up. A girl with red pigtails answered, "They should save a little and spend a little. Compromise."

That's it. These kids were done with that problem. And then: "OK. Next?"

Why is the solution so clear to eight-year-olds, but not to us grown-ups? Here's an answer: We fear that in compromising, we will lose the core of ourselves. Every one of us has a set of beliefs, values, and experiences that we tuck in a secret treasure chest within ourselves. When an issue cracks open the lid of that treasure chest and we face having to compromise, we imagine we'll have to turn over our most deeply held beliefs. This feels like losing the heart of our selves, while letting our partners win everything. We're afraid that we're in a win-lose situation. Furthermore, compromise feels like we may betray ourselves by not asserting what's most important to us. It feels like too much to ask. Compromise may feel like potential surrender. So we resist, we hold our ground, we dig in, and we refuse to give an inch. Eight-year-olds are a little wiser than we are. They see the situation as win-win. And they're right.

When we watched the masters of the transition to parenthood work on solving their problems, there was a trick to it. First, they talked about the core of the issue for each one personally—what they each needed, what they could not yield on. They defined that territory carefully, but also made it as small as possible. Then, feeling safer, they defined what they were flexible about—the parts of the issue that weren't so central to them. Then they felt safe enough to compromise, because their core beliefs were accepted and protected. We call this method the two-circle method of compromise.

Let's take an example. Leroy and Chantel had the very problem we presented to the eight-year-olds. Even Leroy's friends described him as "real tight with money." He admitted it. He had worked hard and saved some money before he met Chantel. He wasn't rich by a long shot, but it was some serious money. Many temptations had come Leroy's way in the past, but he had resisted spending his money, and so it slowly grew. He had seen his friends blow bigger wads of cash on frivolous investments, cars, and big parties. He considered this flashy and superficial.

Chantel and Leroy fought a lot about money. One issue for them was the amount of money they spent on entertainment, and the amount of money they spent on getting help for Chantel after the baby came. They had gone through a period before the baby when Chantel didn't know how to budget, and her spending had been out of control. She had never had a credit card before, and she used it too much. Chantel will admit that. But now she said she was different. She didn't want to live for the future. She wanted to live for now, too. Leroy explained his whole attitude toward money. He said he wanted to buy a house someday. Didn't Chantel want that, too? Yes, she said, she did. OK, Leroy said.

But Chantel came back with memories of how they would go dancing every week, and listen to jazz. Leroy said, "Yes, but that was before the baby came." "Yes," said Chantel, "I know, but it's even more important now for us to be close with each other." "Yes," said Leroy, "but what about the future?" "I know," said Chantel. "Thanks for proving my point," said Leroy. They both laughed.

Then Chantel said, "Leroy, on the one hand, it's save everything, and just pay the bills, never spend anything on fun. On the other hand, it's live it up and save nothing for the future. They're both wrong. Can't you give a little here, compromise, spend a little and save a little?" Leroy rubbed his chin and said, "OK, name me a figure." Chantel said, "You're not going to get all stubborn?" "No, I'm not," said Leroy. "Just name me a figure." Chantel hesitated, looked away, and said, "OK, let's say we spend three hundred bucks a month. That would cover some help for me with the baby so I can go to school, and also cover a few nights out a month, just you and me. How's that?" Leroy frowned and said, "Come down a bit for me here." Chantel looked away again and said, "OK, let's say two hundred bucks a month." Leroy smiled and said, "You got it, baby." Now it was Chantel's turn to smile. She said, "This could lead to a great improvement."

They had built a bridge over an impasse, a bridge to each other. They had been able to follow the advice of the eight-year-olds. They had been able to find their common base of agreement. Leroy felt understood about his core position. Chantel also felt understood about her core position. Then flexibility and compromise was the next order of business. Now Leroy looked at Chantel and said, "I didn't know you wanted to go to school. To do what?" "I'll tell you all about it," said Chantel. They were off and running. Compromise created the goodwill for them to talk about deeper things.

Esther and Danny had another problem. Blessed with twin one-year-olds, family breakfast times were fun but chaotic. Esther didn't like it when the twins threw Cheerios on the floor. She'd bark at them to cut it out. Danny, however, thought it was all just a game, one he wanted to play with them. "Just let 'em have some fun," he crooned.

"But they're not being respectful of the work I have to do to clean up after them," she said.

"Esther, they start to cry when you yell at them."

"I'm *not* yelling," she yelled.

"OK, OK, calm down. Let's see if we can compromise here."

They spoke of how they'd each had very strict upbringings. Esther thought her parents were right in teaching her to respect their limits. But Danny thought otherwise about his childhood. His parents had been too rigid, and he wanted to raise his kids with more fun and fewer rules. In seeking some common ground, they both agreed that they wanted the twins to have limits on certain behaviors and to learn respect for their elders. But was this one of those moments where limits came first, and play, second? They both concurred, "No." Then Danny said, "How about if I do Cheerios duty in the morning and handle breakfast cleanup?"

"Fantastic! How about dinner dishes, too?"

"Forget it!"

"Just thought I'd try." She laughed.

How are your compromising skills as a couple? Take the next self-test together.

SELF-TEST ON COMPROMISE

Read each statement and place a check mark in the appropriate TRUE or FALSE box.

DURING OUR ATTEMPTS TO RESOLVE CONFLICT BETWEEN US . . .	YOU		YOUR PARTNER	
We are usually good at resolving our differences.	T	F	T	F
We both believe in meeting each other halfway when we disagree.	T	F	T	F
In discussing issues, we can usually find our common ground of agreement.	T	F	T	F
Yielding power is not very difficult for me.	T	F	T	F
Give and take in making decisions is not a problem in this relationship.	T	F	T	F

If you each answered at least three out of five of these items "True," then your skills are OK. But try the next exercise anyway, and these skills may improve over time. If either of you answered fewer than three items "True," then you have some work ahead of you. Again, try the next exercise, and your skills will probably improve right away.

EXERCISE

COMPROMISE

To reach a compromise on your issue, you need to first think about what you need on this issue. Define a positive need: What do you hope for or wish for here? If a magic wand could be waved and you could have exactly what you needed, what would that be?

- First, define the smallest, most minimal core area of need each of you cannot yield on. What is your core need here? That will make you feel safe and change the win-lose situation to a win-win situation. Define *what* you need, what you have to have.

- Second, define areas of greater flexibility. This can be *when* or *how* you and your partner get what you each need.

97

▨ Third, come up with a temporary compromise. There are different levels of compromise. Talk about what you can and cannot do on this issue in terms of respecting your spouse's position right now.

Getting to Understanding.

Getting stuck? Ask one another these questions:

▨ How can we each provide emotional support on this issue?

▨ Do you understand why your partner's core areas are so important to him or her? If not, politely say, "Please help me understand what you need and why."

▨ What do we agree about? What goals do we each have? Can we develop a common view here?

▨ How do I better honor your need here?

▨ What common ground can we identify?

▨ What are our common feelings, or the most important feelings here?

▨ What common goals can we have here?

▨ How can we understand this situation, this issue?

▨ How do we think these goals should be accomplished?

▨ What are my areas of flexibility? Can I yield on how fast things happen? Or the extent to which it happens, or the cost, and so on?

Divide Each of Your Positions Into Two Areas:

FLEXIBILITY AREA   INFLEXIBILITY AREA

Write these down after the following statements.

MY CORE AREAS THAT ARE INFLEXIBLE ARE:

MY FLEXIBILITY AREAS ARE:

MY PARTNER'S CORE INFLEXIBILITY AREAS ARE:

MY PARTNER'S FLEXIBILITY AREAS ARE:

8

THE IMPORTANCE OF REPAIR

Remember when we compared communication to baseball? It's no exaggeration that a great batting average in both baseball and communication is .300. That means 70 percent of the time we're sailing right by each other, just like a batter striking out. Our communication often misses the mark.

Worse yet are the times when the words we pitch actually hurt our partners—those nasty retorts we blurt out, or the regrettable insults we hurl just as our partner reaches out. There are those unfortunate times when our partners' bids for attention sail through the empty air. All those misses are completely understandable when we've been up with our babies all night, or when we're too tired to even care how we respond. Our communication then strikes out. Now what?

The answer is simple. When we mess up, we have to fix it. We have to make a repair. A repair is a few words or a gesture that gets our communication back in the ballpark, where we're on the same team again. And it takes both of us for a repair to work.

With John's students Janice Driver and Amber Tabares, we have studied repair processes in relationships for the past seven years. The research has shown us that the master couples handle repairs differently than disaster couples. Partners in successful relationships make and accept each other's repair attempts. In contrast, unsuccessful partners either neglect to make a repair, or if one is made, they rebuff it.

We've also learned that there's no one right way to make a repair. What's more important is that for a repair to work, it has to be made *and* accepted. Let's look at an example.

Jake complained that Janice's parents were planning to visit for three weeks after their baby's birth next month. Janice bristled, "What's wrong with their coming that soon? I'll need all the help I can get."

"But I'll be there to help you."

"You're not enough."

Jake's hackles went up. "Thanks a lot!"

Janice realized her mistake. Backing down, she said, "Oops, I didn't mean that. I know we're a great team, and you're terrific."

Jake softened. "You're right, and thanks for repairing."

"You're welcome . . . Now, about their visiting . . ."

When Janice recognized that she'd insulted Jake, she quickly changed course, reassuring him that she respected and appreciated him and knew they'd be a great team together after Baby's arrival. Jake accepted Janice's repair and thanked her for it, which got them on the right track again. Then they resumed their discussion.

We're all familiar with that crown jewel of repairs, "I'm sorry." Of course, when we say it, we have to really mean it and be willing to change. But there are so many ways of making repairs when our communication crosses the foul line that we are going to give you an entire "repair kit" below. First, let's take a look at a self-test for repair.

SELF-TEST ON EFFECTIVE REPAIR ATTEMPTS

Read each statement and place a check mark in the appropriate TRUE or FALSE box.

DURING OUR ATTEMPTS TO RESOLVE CONFLICT BETWEEN US . . .	YOU		YOUR PARTNER	
We are good at taking breaks when we need them.	T	F	T	F
Even when arguing, we can maintain a sense of humor.	T	F	T	F
We are pretty good listeners even when we have different positions on things.	T	F	T	F
If things get heated, we can usually pull out of it and change things.	T	F	T	F
My partner is good at soothing me when I get upset.	T	F	T	F

If you each answered at least three out of five of these items "True," then your repair skills are OK. But try the next exercise, and these repair skills may improve even more over time. If either of you answered "True" in fewer than three items, then you have some work ahead of you. The next exercise should help you create some repair skills right away.

EXERCISE

EFFECTIVE REPAIR

INSTRUCTIONS. The next time you have a conversation, keep this list in front of you. Read it over before you begin. Then, if your conversation gets offtrack, pick an item from the list of repair statements below that you think is an appropriate repair for this moment and say it out loud to your partner. If you are hearing the repair, try your best to accept it, and then go on with your conversation accordingly. Here's what it might sound like, when both husband and wife make repairs.

Example:

HUSBAND: I forgot to pick up the tickets to the game today.

WIFE: You're so forgetful. What's the matter with you?

HUSBAND, *after looking over the list:* Hmmm. Number twenty-nine. I feel defensive. Can you rephrase that?

WIFE: Oops. Number three. I really blew that one. I'm just disappointed that we don't have the tickets yet.

HUSBAND: Me, too.

Potential Repair Statements

1. My reactions were too extreme. I'm sorry.
2. I might be wrong here.
3. I really blew that one.
4. Please, let's stop for a while.
5. Let me try again.
6. That must have really hurt your feelings.
7. I apologize. I was flooded and should have taken a break.
8. Talk to me about what you're feeling.
9. How can I make this better?
10. I want to be gentler to you right now.
11. Let's start all over again.
12. I can see my part in all this.
13. Let's agree to disagree here.
14. Hang in there. Don't withdraw.
15. Let me start again in a softer way.
16. I'm sorry. Please forgive me.
17. I really need to calm down.
18. I really got scared. Can you make things safer for me?
19. Help me to say things more gently.
20. Did I do something wrong?
21. I need your support right now.
22. That hurt my feelings.
23. Just listen to me right now and try to understand.

24. Tell me you love me.

25. I'm feeling sad. Can you please comfort me?

26. Can I have a kiss?

27. I am feeling unappreciated.

28. Please be gentler with me.

29. I feel defensive. Can you rephrase that?

30. Please help me calm down.

31. Please don't lecture me.

32. Please be quiet and listen to me. Let me talk until I say I'm done.

33. I don't feel like you understand

34. This is important to me. Please listen to me right now.

35. I need to finish what I was saying.

36. Please don't withdraw.

37. You were starting to convince me, but I interrupted the process.

38. I know this isn't your fault.

39. I agree with part of what you're saying.

40. Can we talk again? I realize what my part of this problem is.

41. Let's compromise here.

42. Let's find our common ground.

43. Thank you for . . .

44. I never thought of things that way.

45. I really do think your point of view makes sense.

46. I love you. Let's work on this.

47. Let's agree to include both our views in a solution.

9

THE AFTERMATH OF A FIGHT: PROCESS AND UNDERSTAND IT

Together, we give couples workshops for three hundred to four hundred people at a time. In every one, we discuss a fight we've just had—and we're never at a loss for a doozy. It just goes to show, we're in the same soup as everyone else. And it's one that gets boiling hot at times! Here's an example.

One morning soon after our daughter was born, John was in the bathroom, thinking, "This is going to be a good day." Then Julie came in and mumbled, half asleep, "I just had a terrible dream." John said, "I'm in a hurry today, but go ahead, what did you dream?" Julie described how, in her dream, she was still big with child. John had been cold and angry toward her. He'd also been flirting with other women. "Oh, that's an awful dream. I'm so sorry," John said. John tried his best to soothe her, but when she left the bathroom he started to think about her dream. He ended up seething.

John realized that he had consoled Julie by apologizing for what he had done in the dream. "What an idiot I am," he later thought, "I didn't actually do any of that. I don't flirt. Her imagination did those things, not me. This is a problem she's had since the baby arrived. Don't we have enough problems during the day without her going to sleep and dreaming up more problems? And is this dream saying what she really thinks of me? After all I do around here? The nerve."

By the time Julie returned to the bathroom, John had worked himself up into a lather. Now he *was* cold and angry. He announced his feelings, and after that he felt a lot better, and he thought, "This is going to be a good day after all"—that is, until he heard Julie sobbing in the shower.

John got into the shower and tried to put his arms around Julie. She said, "Don't touch me. Just leave me alone. You sound just like the person I dreamed about." John hastily got out of the shower, dried off, and thought, "I guess this isn't going to be such a good day."

We gulped down breakfast in silence and left for work.

That evening, Julie eyed John and muttered, "Do you want to talk?" Squaring off, John grumbled, "Do you?"

"I think we should."

John sulked. "OK."

Fortunately, we had already watched lots of master couples discussing how they'd fought so we had a blueprint for how to do it right. We call this strategy of processing a fight the "aftermath of a fight."

We sat down over some hot coffee (necessary only if you're from Seattle). One at a time, we listened to each other's feelings and points of view on our debacle. Then we each confessed our role in the mess we made. Next we cited one thing we could each do to avoid war the next time Julie had one of those dreams. Last, we unearthed what had triggered each of us to fire on each other.

Here's what we came up with.

1. FEELINGS. After reflecting on Julie's dream, John felt unjustly accused, righteously indignant, and furious. And after John's words, Julie felt crushed, alienated and alone, and wanted to run. She also felt ugly and unlikable.

Now, we didn't argue about whether or not our feelings were justified or reasonable. We just accepted them for the natural responses they were.

2. POINTS OF VIEW. Julie explained that this dream was only symbolic in nature, and wasn't meant to be taken personally. Old feelings of insecurity were surfacing, and because she needed John's love the most, he got to represent the current "rejecter" in her dream. But instead of trying to understand the dream (like any psychologist should), John took it to be about him personally and grew defensive, angry, and attacking. Unfortunately, John shape-shifted in that moment into the kind of person Julie feared the most.

On the other hand, John felt that this dream exposed Julie's hidden unconscious feelings about him. He worried that Julie viewed him as unfaithful. But that made him really angry. He didn't deserve such a smear, especially when he'd been so kind and loving lately. For that matter, he wasn't hearing much appreciation for all the cooking he'd done, either.

At this point, we simply "validated" one another by admitting that each other's perceptions made some sense to us.

3. ADMITTING OUR ROLE. Each of us owned up to not being halo-topped angels. Julie went first. She admitted that she'd taken John for granted lately and neglected to thank him for all he was doing around the house. Since lecturing to huge groups clashed with her introverted nature, her new role in the spotlight had fired up old insecurities. So maybe she'd thought only of getting support for herself, and didn't think about the effect on John of hearing he was the villain in her dream.

Next, John confessed that he'd felt depressed lately. Several of his research grants hadn't been funded, so he was edgy and stressed out. Just maybe he had taken things too personally. Then he had stopped being Dr. Jekyll, and become Mr. Hyde.

4. MAKING IT BETTER NEXT TIME. Julie said that next time she dreamed of John as a bad guy, she could forewarn him that she didn't really see him that way. These were her anxieties piping up again. She would also watch for the good things John was doing and thank him for them. Grinning, John replied that an intro would go a long way toward enabling him to hear what a louse he'd been in her dream.

John wanted to do better at comforting Julie after dreams like this one, but he didn't know what she might need at those times, though anger definitely wasn't it. Julie couldn't give him a formula. She suggested that he ask about her needs in the moment, because at that time, she'd know them better.

They shook on it.

But let's be honest with you. Processing this fight didn't smooth out our next battle. We don't expect that it will. The next fight we had was over something John's mother had said: a brand-new issue. So we spun out again, committed a few "fouls," and had to process a new fight. That's what most couples do—cycle through a variety of issues with a few flat tires along the way. But ultimately, when we can process our fights well, we emerge with a deeper understanding of our partner's humanity, the jagged edges they grapple with inside themselves. And by grasping our partners' points of view on specific issues, we can avoid spinning our wheels when we hit that issue again.

On to the specifics. A brilliant psychotherapist named Dan Wile explained that we have to get outside the fight in order to process it and leave it behind. This means *not* getting back in the ring and duking out Round 12 of an endless boxing match. We have to calm down and stay out of the ring. Only then can we get some emotional distance from the fight and see it more objectively. We also have to drop our gloves and become peacemakers.

It's like watching an instant replay of our match on TV. For us to learn something, it's got to be in slow motion. Then, together, we can calmly stand outside the ring, see what went wrong, and know what better moves to make next time.

First, we have to identify the perceptions, feelings, and thoughts that arose in us during the fight. And as you know, there will always be two points of view in every fight. It's crucial that we understand our partner's point of view, attempt to make sense of it, and convey that to our partner. After this is accomplished, we can shed our boxing gloves and gently talk over what happened.

Next, we get down to the hard part. We each have to take some responsibility for our part in the fight. Nobody likes doing this. But when we do, the problem becomes *our* problem in communicating, and not the diabolical dealings of Lex Luthor, who, of course, is our partner, and not ourselves. Arguments are almost never one person's fault.

We are talking about discussions and conflict discussions about disagreements, not physical violence. There's no justification for anyone being a victim of violence. If the batterer does not agree to make profound changes, the partner must leave. Ensuring our own safety and the survival of our children is our own ultimate responsibility.

The following exercise will provide you with clear guidance on how to process a fight. Remember, we can't recover when there's only blame and defensiveness. But we can melt away hurt and anger when we acknowledge our own human frailties and foibles and agree to try harder next time.

EXERCISE

PROCESSING THE AFTERMATH OF A FIGHT

INSTRUCTIONS. Discuss the last fight you had using the following questions as your guide. Take turns answering each question, but tell your partner your answers rather than circling them. Alternate answering each question. For example, the first question is about what you felt during the fight. Read aloud the feelings on the list that were true for you. Next, listen to your partner's feelings from the list. Then go on to the next question. When it comes to admitting your role, be sure you're calm before getting started so you can avoid getting back into the fight. If the fight erupts again, stop, take a thirty-minute break, self-soothe, and then try again, taking up where you left off.

Describe the Feelings You Had During the Fight

Read over the list of negative and positive feelings below and state aloud which feelings you had while your partner listens. Don't explain why you had those feelings—just name them. Then trade roles and listen while your partner does the same.

Negative Feelings

1. I felt defensive.
2. During the argument my feelings got hurt.
3. I felt excluded.
4. I felt angry.
5. I felt sad.
6. I felt misunderstood.
7. I felt criticized.
8. I felt like my partner didn't even like me.
9. I was afraid.
10. I was worried.
11. I felt I was right and my partner was wrong.
12. I felt out of control.
13. I felt righteously indignant.
14. I felt unfairly picked on.
15. I felt unappreciated.
16. I felt unattractive.
17. I felt neglected.
18. I felt disgusted.
19. I was disapproving.
20. I was morally outraged.
21. I felt taken for granted.
22. I felt like leaving.
23. I was overwhelmed with emotion.
24. I felt powerless.

25. I felt like I had no influence.

26. I felt like my opinions didn't even matter.

27. I had no feelings at all.

28. I had no idea what I was feeling.

29. Other feelings:

Positive Feelings

1. I felt calm.

2. I felt loved.

3. I felt appreciated.

4. I felt respected.

5. I felt happy.

6. I felt powerful.

7. I felt loving.

8. I felt kind.

9. I felt in control.

10. I felt like we were making progress.

11. I felt connected to my partner.

12. I felt optimistic.

13. Other feelings:

Next, summarize your own point of view in this argument while your part-ner listens. Then listen while your partner does the same. Avoid blaming your partner, disagreeing with your partner, or getting back into the fight. Instead, step into your partner's shoes and try to see how your partner's point of view might make sense, given your partner's perspective.

Now, communicate your understanding in words to your partner.

Admit Your Role in the Fight

To stop being defensive, attacking, or critical, you need to first understand *your* part in creating this fight. Like all of us, you'd like to think that this fight is all your partner's fault. But usually it isn't; on the other hand, it isn't all your fault, either.

Instead, you've both created a cycle, a dynamic between you in which you've each played a role. But it's too critical to tell your partner what he or she has done wrong. It works much better to admit your own role, even if it's a small one.

Make sure you're calm first. If you're not, take at least a twenty-minute break and then reconvene. During your break, practice the five steps of self-soothing to help yourself: (1) breathe evenly and deeply, (2) tense and then relax each muscle group, (3) feel each muscle group getting heavy, (4) feel each muscle group getting warm, and (5) visualize your personal image of tranquillity and peace. Also, let go of negative thoughts that maintain your distress, like how you're being misunderstood or victimized, or feeling righteously indignant. Calmer? Now continue.

Look over this list. Any of them fit, even a little? If so, tell your partner.

1. I have been stressed and irritable lately.

2. I have not expressed much appreciation toward my partner lately.

3. I have taken my partner for granted.

4. I have been overly sensitive lately.

5. I have been overly critical lately.

6. I have not shared very much of my inner world with my partner.

7. I have not been emotionally available to my partner lately.

8. I have been more typically turning away from my partner.

9. I have been getting easily upset.

10. I have been depressed lately.

11. I've had a chip on my shoulder lately.

12. I have not been very affectionate.

13. I have not made time for good things between us.

14. I have not been a very good listener lately.

15. I have not asked for what I need.

16. I have been feeling a bit like a martyr.

17. Other:

Next, describe overall your contribution to this fight.

How Can You Make This Better in the Future?

Gently tell your partner one thing he or she could do differently next time to avoid fighting over this issue.

Now say one thing that you could do differently to improve your next discussion on this issue.

By carefully following the outline above, you can walk away from that argument feeling closer to one another. Even better, your next conversation on this issue may not be an argument at all.

10

PROCESSING A FIGHT: DEEPENING YOUR UNDERSTANDING

Fred and Marley were success stories before they married. Fred had driven a truck for many years before he finally bought his own hauler. Now he owned a fleet of trucks and was the CEO of his own company. Good thing, too, because he had never been good at working for someone else. For the first few months, he might be fine. But then his boss would supervise him with a little "constructive criticism." Furious and defensive, Fred would quit. "My supervisors were always idiots. They always knew a lot less than I did, but they'd get on a power trip and try to control me," he said.

Fred's problems with authority circled back to childhood. Early on, his parents had decided: no children. But later, annoyingly, along came Fred. He was an active boy. His parents often dryly informed him that he had destroyed their peaceful life. Fred hated their icy authority and rebelled. So they carted him off to boarding school. It was a militaristic and regimented outpost, and Fred detested it, but there was no escape. His parents had jailed him there for eight years. Even now, with all he'd achieved, Fred still felt the sting of his parents' disdain. They would always see him as the bad boy.

Marley was a successful graphic artist in Seattle. Locally acclaimed, she had pocketed many big-name contracts. But she, too, had agonized during childhood. Her biological father abandoned the family when she was a baby. A year later, her mother remarried a traumatized and violent veteran of Vietnam. He railed at Marley. If she didn't kowtow to him, he slapped her. Sometimes he backhanded her because she happened to be standing next to him. Marley's mother bent her back to his will and shrugged off Marley's tears. Emotionally exiled, Marley felt frightened and alone. To this day, Marley still shuddered at the staccato of an angry voice or loud noise.

Both lonely, reclusive, and driven, Fred and Marley met in their late thirties. Sensing kinship in one another, they quickly married, and a year later, Sammy was born. Fred didn't dare leave his company, so Marley referred out her clients and took maternity leave. She adored nurturing Sammy and funneled her creativity into remodeling the house.

But since Sammy's birth a year and a half earlier, Fred hadn't appreciated Marley's many sacrifices. She felt taken for granted, and conflict between them skyrocketed. And though Marley personally loathed a nag, she found herself sounding like one. "You don't do one thing around this house," she repeated like a broken record.

One wintry morning, Marley came downstairs with the baby. Fred was already in the kitchen. He'd let out the cat and was now toasting his English muffin. Lowering Sammy gently to the floor, Marley barked, "Fred, you left the door open. Come here and close it."

Fred snapped back, "You've got to be kidding. You're standing right next to the door. Just close it yourself."

"But I didn't open it."

"If it's so damn important to you, you close it."

"No. That's your job."

"Don't be ridiculous. You're such a bitch."

At that point, Marley stomped out of the kitchen, threw open every window downstairs, folded her arms across her chest, and stared, blazing, at Fred. Fred ran from room to room screaming invectives and slamming every window shut. Stunned, Marley went silent, and Sammy wound up and wailed in fear. After a long moment, Marley scooped him up, slung him on her hip, and marched toward the stairs. As she ascended with a look of disgust on her face, she glared over her shoulder. "How could you?"

Now, this is a fight worth analyzing. Isn't it amazing how such seemingly trivial issues can lead to Dunkirk? Psychologist Dan Wile explains that every fight contains hidden conversations that lie dormant underground. If the couple had these discussions instead, they wouldn't need this fight. Our research shows that Wile is right.

What conversations did Fred and Marley need to have? The answer is tucked away in their childhoods and current circumstances. Marley needed to talk to Fred about how unappreciated she had felt since she'd exchanged her pens and pencils for diapers and aprons. And when he left all the housework, child care, laundry, and cooking up to her, she felt abandoned and disrespected. Furthermore, when he added to the ever-present mess, she wanted to go ballistic. But she also hated to nag him. In fact, asking him or anyone for anything felt terribly difficult to do. Seeing how she'd gotten nothing in childhood, she didn't think she deserved help now. Nonetheless, her resentment at doing all the work alone had piled up. Now, becoming a drill sergeant was her only option if she wanted help. She really didn't know another way to ask for what she needed.

Meanwhile, Fred needed to say how overwhelmed he was by marriage, new fatherhood, and the roller-coaster ride of work. He wanted to be a good husband to Marley, even if that meant helping around the house, a decidedly unmasculine role for him. But he knew nothing about housework, cooking, or fathering, for that matter. After all, during most of his childhood, the janitors had done the cleanup work. And sadly, no father figures existed in that world to serve as role models for him now. He didn't mind helping out as long as Marley gently instructed him on what to do.

However, when she got that harsh tone in her voice? He couldn't stand it. It reminded him of every forced crew cut he'd ever had, every jut-jawed, dead-hearted teacher who'd slapped him every time he muttered one wrong word. He just couldn't take it. Gentle requests were one thing. Angry demands, quite another.

So putting it all together, what triggered these two to fight? Marley was first angered by Fred's implicit expectation that she close the door that he had left open. She felt treated like a maid, disrespected. Thus, her demand that Fred close the door. But when Fred rebelled and then slammed around the house cursing, she became terrified. The gunshot noises of windows banging around ricocheted her back to her childhood home, where her father's unpredictable blows had assailed her. But her fear quickly crystallized into contempt for the tantrum-throwing two-year-old her husband had become. Thus, her parting shot, "How could you?"

Of course, Fred hated being bossed around. He'd been peacefully and methodically starting his day. But turning around, he faced not a wife but a hag who wanted to humiliate and control him. All she needed to do was reach over two feet and tap the door closed. How insane that she demanded him to, like some master ordering his dog around. He'd taken that for years, but wasn't about to now. But the more he resisted, the more insistent she became. Meanwhile, deep below the surface, he heard the rumbles of his parents whispering, "Disgusting boy. I wish he'd dry up and blow away." Then, calm and cool behavior no longer mattered. He'd show her.

For Fred and Marley to understand this fight and deepen their compassion for one another, they would need to vent those underground pressures. Marley would need to tell Fred how his storming around the house triggered her memories of being assaulted, and how frightened she'd become. Her contempt at the end was only a cover-up for her fear. And Fred would need to say how her style of making demands reminded him of all the orders he'd taken, first from his parents and later his teachers, and how those orders contained no concern or love for him, that he was commanded to obey and nothing more. In the kitchen, he'd felt shrunken, shamed, and flooded by thirty years of rage. Not so much about her, but about the years of derision he'd taken. A discussion like this would help Fred and Marley to see each other as wounded and struggling for dignity, rather than as dark villains ready to maim each other.

For this couple to avoid the shoals of battle, they would have had to have a different discussion to begin with. Here's what it could have sounded like.

MARLEY: Honey, I'm upset that you left the door open. It's cold in here. Would you mind closing it?

FRED: How about you doing it? You're right next to the door.

MARLEY: Right. But you know, I feel like a maid sometimes when I need to complete something that you began, like opening and shutting the door. How come you didn't close it, anyway?

FRED: Well, actually I was a little hot from my shower. I figured I'd cool off and shut it later.

MARLEY: Oh. But when we're about to come downstairs, why don't you go outside to cool off so we can come into a nice warm kitchen?

FRED: Sounds doable.

Looks pretty easy. But what if they started to get into it? Here's a shortcut around the rocks:

MARLEY: Fred, come over here and close the door.

FRED: Wait a minute, Marley. When you talk to me like that, I hear Dad, military school, those idiot teachers—all of it. Would you mind talking to me with more respect? You know how I hate being bossed around.

MARLEY: Oh, I didn't realize I was doing that. Sorry. But I've got a gripe, too. I'm freezing in here, and Sammy isn't dressed warm enough for a cold kitchen. I don't see why I should be the one to have to close the door when you left it open. It makes me feel like the butler or something.

FRED: Good point. Incidentally, thanks for cleaning up in here last night.

MARLEY: Thanks. But would you please close the door anyway? Wife, yes. Butler, no.

FRED: OK, OK *(laughing)*.

Instead of colliding with abusive name-calling and making countercommands, Fred and Marley call out to each other from within their own vulnerabilities. Fred informs Marley that his emotional scars are being sliced open by the razor in her voice. And she takes heed. But she doesn't retreat completely. She still has a complaint to voice. She just softens her tone so he can hear her better. Their exchange is a simple one. But above all, it's respectful. And because Fred's explosion is short-circuited, Marley is protected from her own demons surfacing.

When we stay mindful of our partners' sensitivities yet state our needs clearly, we can skirt around our sharp words and have caring conversations instead. Talking about what psychologist Thomas Bradbury calls "enduring vulnerabilities" is essential for Fred and Marley. They need to identify what triggered them and made them go ballistic. Then they need to understand why these are their triggers.

One way to see where your vulnerabilities lie is by processing a fight you've had and examining its deeper layers. Think of a recent fight you've had. Was ancient history unearthed in you? Did your partner inadvertently trip over a crack in you that you've kept camouflaged? Did your partner's behavior somehow remind you of someone else who has hurt you in the past? Some past betrayal or loss that still aches today? Or do you have triggers that you need to warn your partner about so they can be avoided?

The next exercise will help you to deepen your understanding of a fight you've had.

DEEPENING THE AFTERMATH OF A FIGHT

INSTRUCTIONS. Here is a guide for evaluating what happened in your last fight and increasing your compassion for each other. This form is designed to help you talk about a fight without getting back into it, and to make your next conversation on this issue more constructive. Think of a fight you'd like to discuss with your partner. First, make sure you've talked about all the points covered in the exercise in chapter 9. Then go on to the following questions and, one by one, write down your answers privately. Then discuss them with your partner. Try not to get back into the fight. Remember, there is no absolute "reality" in a marital conflict, but only two points of view that are both valid in their own ways. You are answering two questions: 1) What were the triggers for each of you? and 2) Why are those your triggers?

WHAT WERE THE TRIGGERS THAT MADE THIS FIGHT HARD FOR YOU?

WERE THE TRIGGERS RELATED TO YOUR FEELING EXCLUDED?

Circle how much you felt the following feelings.

	A GREAT DEAL	DEFINITELY	A LITTLE	NOT AT ALL
1. I felt excluded.	___	___	___	___
2. No one was interested in me.	___	___	___	___
3. I felt ignored.				
4. I felt unimportant to my partner.	___	___	___	___
5. I felt cold toward my partner.	___	___	___	___
6. My partner was not happy to see me.	___	___	___	___
7. Others (write in):	___	___	___	___

DID THE TRIGGERS RELATE TO YOUR FEELING THE LOSS OF AFFECTION?

Circle how much you felt the following feelings.

	A GREAT DEAL	DEFINITELY	A LITTLE	NOT AT ALL
1. I felt no affection toward me.	___	___	___	___
2. I experienced my partner as cold toward me.	___	___	___	___
3. I definitely felt rejected.	___	___	___	___
4. I felt criticized.	___	___	___	___
5. I felt no affection toward my partner.	___	___	___	___
6. I felt that my partner was not attracted to me.	___	___	___	___
7. Others (write in): _____	___	___	___	___

WERE THE TRIGGERS RELATED TO YOUR FEELING THAT YOU HAD NO INFLUENCE?

Circle how much you had the following feelings.

	A GREAT DEAL	DEFINITELY	A LITTLE	NOT AT ALL
1. I had no power in this discussion.	___	___	___	___
2. I felt helpless to affect how the conversation went.	___	___	___	___
3. I felt there was a lack of respect toward me.	___	___	___	___
4. My sense of dignity was being compromised.	___	___	___	___

122

	A GREAT DEAL	DEFINITELY	A LITTLE	NOT AT ALL
5. My partner felt domineering to me.	___	___	___	___
6. I could not persuade my partner at all.	___	___	___	___
7. Others (write in): _____	___	___	___	___

Now share your answers with your partner. Then see if you can understand their connections with your past. Do they remind you of experiences you've had before? What kind of experiences? If so, try to discuss them with your partner. Some difficult reflection may be necessary here. Can you identify particular issues that trigger experiences and feelings like these? How would you like to handle them differently in the future?

Summing up your answers above, what is the conversation you needed to have instead of the fight? Discuss your answers together and write them down below.

I NEEDED TO TALK TO MY PARTNER ABOUT:

MY PARTNER NEEDED TO TALK TO ME ABOUT:

11

UNSOLVABLE PROBLEMS: MOVE FROM GRIDLOCK TO DIALOGUE

Do you have problems that never get solved? They circle back around like a dog chasing its tail? When we brought back couples to our lab, we found that, except for their clothes and hairstyles, our couples were raising the same issues year after year. They looked different, but their problems didn't. When we analyzed these sessions, we were stunned. A whopping 69 percent of the problems were repeats. Perpetual and irritating, they were fleas that refused to die, driving that dog crazy.

Year after year, perpetual problems nag us. They stem from our fundamental differences in personality, lifestyle, or needs; traits that are embedded in us. You're punctual but I'm not. You love people but I'm shy. You're neat but I'm messy. You're frugal but I'm spendy. You love together-time but I love independence. You're emotionally volatile but I'm detached. You treasure affection but I need space. These characteristics define each of us; they're like our bones. Our bones may not be shaped perfectly. They may creak when we get up in the morning. They may be sharp and pointed and an imperfect fit with our partners' bones. But ultimately they hold us up. They ARE who we are. So there's no way we'll surrender them. Even if it means we bang into our partner over and over again.

We know that when we choose a partner, we're also selecting our relationship issues for, hopefully, the next fifty years. If we picked another person, we might escape these particular problems. But then we'd face different ones, eternally.

Our dear friend Dan Wile writes, "Choosing a partner is choosing a set of problems." For example:

> Paul married Alice and Alice gets loud at parties and Paul, who is shy, hates that. But if Paul had married Susan, he and Susan would have gotten into a fight before they even got to the party. That's because Paul is always late and Susan hates to be kept waiting. She would feel taken for granted, which she is very sensitive about. Paul would see her complaining about this as her attempt to dominate him, which he is very sensitive about. If Paul had married Gail, they wouldn't have even gone to the party because they would still be upset about an argument they had the day before about Paul's not helping with the housework. To Gail, when Paul does not help she feels abandoned, which she is sensitive about, and to Paul, Gail's complaining is an attempt at domination, which he is sensitive about. The same is true about Alice. If she had married Steve, she would have the opposite problem, because Steve gets drunk at parties and she would get so angry at his drinking that they would get into a fight about it. If she had married Lou, she and Lou would have enjoyed the party but then when they got home the trouble would begin when Lou wanted sex because he always wants sex when he wants to feel closer, but sex is something Alice only wants when she already feels close.

We gravitate toward our perpetual issues especially when we're overworked and exhausted, in short, after we have babies. Then it's harder to deal with them because we lack the energy to stop scratching at them—and at each other.

Here's an example. Peter was raised in a home with six other siblings. With parental attention split seven ways, no child got much. All the kids worked hard at home, making the beds immediately after rising in the morning, taking turns doing the dishes, and babysitting the younger sibs. At birthday time, each child got a card and a small present. That was it. Peter had wanted more, but he came to accept this as his due.

Meanwhile, Jill was an only child. Her parents hired a house-keeper, so Jill did virtually no chores growing up. For birthdays, her parents hosted big parties with her favorite dessert, chocolate fudge cake, a clown to do the entertaining, sometimes a pony, and lots of presents.

Now married, Peter and Jill fight like cats and dogs, especially about keeping the house tidy and how much to give their baby as she grows up. Jill feels criticized by Peter for her "casual" approach to housework, while Peter thinks he does too big a share of the housework. Jill wants to shower Baby with gifts, while Peter thinks that will spoil her. They'll have these perpetual issues forever, because their lifestyle choices are embedded with completely different family histories and values.

What are the perpetual issues in your relationship? Take the next self-test and see. First, here's a rule to follow. If only one of you thinks an issue is perpetual, then it is.

EXERCISE

YOUR PERPETUAL ISSUES

INSTRUCTIONS. Look over each item. Check the box next to the item number if you think it is one of your perpetual issues. You may add other items if you wish.

Remember, perpetual problems arise from (1) fundamental differences in your personalities or (2) fundamental differences in your lifestyle needs that create conflict.

☐ *Differences in neatness and organization.* One of you is neat and organized and the other is sloppy and disorganized.

☐ *Differences in emotionality.* One of you is very emotionally expressive and the other is not so expressive. One of you also values exploring one's emotions more than the other.

127

- *Differences in wanting time together versus time apart and alone.* One of you wants more time alone than the other one, who wants more time together. These reflect basic differences in wanting autonomy versus interdependence.

- *Differences in optimal sexual frequency.* One of you wants sex more often than the other.

- *Differences in preferred lovemaking style.* There are differences in what the two of you want from lovemaking. For example, one of you sees intimacy as a precondition to making love, while the other sees love-making as a path to intimacy.

- *Differences in approaching finances.* One of you is much more financially conservative and a worrier, while the other wants to spend a lot more than the other, and has a philosophy more of living for the moment.

- *Differences with respect to kin.* One of you wants more independence from kin, and the other wants more closeness.

- *Differences in how to approach household chores.* For example, one of you wants equal division of labor, while the other does not.

- *Differences in how to raise and discipline children.* One of you is more involved with the children than the other.

- *Differences in how to raise and discipline children.* One of you is stricter with the children than another.

- *Differences in how to raise and discipline children.* One of you wants more gentleness and understanding with the children than the other.

- *Differences In punctuality.* One of you is habitually late, but for the other one, it is important to be on time.

- *Differences in preferred activity level.* One of you prefers active physical recreation while the other is more passive and sedentary.

- *Differences in being people oriented.* One of you is more extroverted and gregarious than the other one.

- *Differences in preferred influence.* One of you prefers to be more dominant in decision making than the other one.

- *Differences in ambition and the importance of work.* One of you is far more ambitious and oriented toward work and success than the other one.

▓ *Differences with respect to religion.* One of you values religious principles more than the other one.

▓ *Differences with respect to drugs and alcohol.* One of you is far more tolerant of drugs and alcohol than the other one.

▓ *Differences about money.* For example, one of you feels a greater need to save; the other, a greater need to spend money.

▓ *Differences in independence.* One person feels a greater need to be independent or connected than the other one.

▓ *Differences in excitement.* One person feels a greater need to have life be exciting or adventurous than the other one.

▓ *Differences in preferred style of life.* There are major differences in the way we choose to live life on an everyday basis.

▓ *Differences in values.* There are major differences in what we value in life.

▓ *Differences in marital fidelity.* There are major differences in how loyal sexually or romantically we want to be, or have been, to one another.

▓ *Others.* You supply them here: _____

Discuss with one another which issues you each checked.

Couples who do best with perpetual issues learn to dialogue about them. Think of a chronic condition that we adapt to, but never cure, like irritable bowel syndrome or an achy back. Occasionally, it crops up and we need to lie down and rest, or get some medicine. Dialogue on perpetual issues is like that. We may have a good, solid talk about our issue, and all is well for a while. But next week or next month, it may pop up again. And we need to talk again. And so the issue lives on, year after year. Our ability to dialogue about it is indispensable so that we can live with our problem and make the best of it.

But what happens if we can't dialogue? Then our conflict becomes *gridlocked.* We become entrenched, like a wheel bogged down in a rut. There's no accepting influence from our partner. We get frustrated. We want our partner to say, "You're absolutely right, dear." Instead, we give and take only barbs and jabs. We vilify and attack each other. The one word we link up with "him" or "her" is "selfish."

We pay a high price for gridlock. We end up feeling that our partner doesn't even like us, let alone love us. After a while, all our discussions lack humor, affection, curiosity, empathy, and even basic understanding.

AND **BABY** MAKES **THREE**

We know a couple who was gridlocked over religion. The husband did not believe in God and wanted nothing to do with the church his wife attended. She was deeply religious, though, so she went to church alone. But once they had a baby, she wanted their child to grow up and be confirmed in her church. He wouldn't hear of it. He railed that he didn't want his son to become a sheep who blindly follows religious dogma. She heard insult; was he calling her dogmatic? Every time they talked about this issue, the verbal blows worsened, until they finally gave up talking altogether. Within months, they drifted apart. Now all they could think of was divorce. They couldn't find a way to dialogue toward peace. The only magnet holding them together was their baby.

Many of us trip over gridlocked problems like these and fall down. Or we avoid talking about them and grow warily distant. We can't seem to find a way to talk like friends. If we did, we'd accept our partners as they are and be grateful for what they offer us. Instead, we fantasize about the perfect relationship—for example, cloning ourselves as a member of the opposite sex. (We are perfect, after all.)

Lest we think, though, that our ideal partner exists out there, listen to what Woody Allen says. In one of his films, he is searching for the perfect woman. He finds one with a perfect body, but her brain is very limited. Then he finds another with the perfect brain, but he finds her body unattractive. So he gets a famous neurosurgeon to perform a delicate operation in which the brains are switched. He now has one woman with the perfect body and the perfect brain, and a second woman with an imperfect body and an imperfect brain. Then he proceeds to fall in love with the second woman!

Accepting our partner, with all of his or her limitations, is the key to dialoguing about our perpetual problems. Another angle on acceptance comes from a famous Zen story. A student asks his master why he never married. The master says, "Oh, I was looking for the perfect woman."

The student nods and says, "So, you never found her."

The master says, "Oh, yes. I found her."

"Then, why didn't you marry her?" asks the student.

"Unfortunately, she was looking for the perfect man."

Next, let's see if any of your perpetual issues are gridlocked. Take the next two self-tests to find out. The four horsemen—criticism, defensiveness, contempt, and stonewalling—stampeding your conflict discussions is a good indicator that you're gridlocked.

SELF-TEST ON THE FOUR HORSEMEN

Read each statement and place a check mark in the appropriate TRUE or FALSE box.

WHEN WE DISCUSS OUR ISSUES . . .	YOU		YOUR PARTNER	
I have to defend myself because the charges against me are so unfair.	T	F	T	F
I often feel unappreciated by my partner.	T	F	T	F
My partner doesn't face issues responsibly and maturely.	T	F	T	F
I am just not guilty of many of the things I get accused of.	T	F	T	F
My partner has a lot of trouble being rational and logical.	T	F	T	F

If either of you answered "True" to more than two items, there is a good chance that you are gridlocked. Take the next self-test to be sure.

SELF-TEST ON GRIDLOCK ON PERPETUAL ISSUES

Read each statement and place a check mark in the appropriate TRUE or FALSE box.

WHEN WE DISCUSS OUR ISSUES . . .	YOU		YOUR PARTNER	
We keep hurting each other whenever we discuss our core issues.	T	F	T	F
My partner has a long list of basically unreasonable demands.	T	F	T	F
I don't feel respected when we disagree.	T	F	T	F
My partner often acts in a selfish manner.	T	F	T	F
When we discuss our issues, my partner acts as if I am totally wrong and he or she is totally right.	T	F	T	F

Did either of you answer any of these items "True"? If so, then you have gridlock.

Don't worry. Lots of couples struggle with gridlock. We'll help you cool down gridlock and cook up dialogue instead. A dialogue is a conversation about a perpetual issue that tastes good going down, like warm bread. One essential ingredient is acceptance of the problem. We need to be able to knead the problem, to push and pull at it. And we have to sing our partner's praises but whisper our wish for change. Of course, it helps if we season our dialogue with a little laughter and affection. Sound impossible? Here's a great example, straight from our lab. She wants him to talk more when he is upset about something. And he wants her to spend less money and be more concerned about their bills. They have two perpetual issues. She starts off with a little humor.

> **She:** OK, now. Back to the communication problem. What do you feel about that? Tell me. Tell me your inner feelings. (*Laughs.*)
>
> HE, *laughing:* Like I said, a lot of times . . . I don't know . . . I've always been quiet.
>
> **She:** Is it just because you don't have nothing to talk about, or is it because you don't want to talk about it? Or is it because I'm not saying anything at the moment?

She has put herself down a little to soften her complaint about him. It works.

HE: I don't know. A lot of times, I don't know.

She: I mean, what's the sense in going out . . . OK, example.

Now she is going to soften things again by giving him a concrete example. He likes that and is used to it.

HE: Uh-huh.

She: When we went to Lake Mobie. I mean, I can understand that you couldn't find your way around and everything. That was fine. That's understandable. But it still doesn't hurt to open your lips, you know? (She is laughing, and so is he.)

HE: I was kind of burned out that day. I was thinking about bills. I didn't want to talk to you about the bills.

She: OK, I'm glad you didn't. (She laughs, and so does he.) But say we're coming from the hospital or something like that. Talk to me about your feelings. OK, I don't even mind you talking about the bills, but like I said, we're not going to worry about the bills. We'll pay what we can pay. Don't worry about it.

HE: Yeah, but you don't seem to understand. Every time I tell you, this is when the trouble first starts.

She: What? When we don't worry about the bills?

HE: Yeah. This is what I'm steadily trying to pound into you.

His perpetual issue is now on the table. She expresses her philosophy.

She: Yeah, but we can only pay what we can pay, so why worry about—

HE: 'Cause that's how I am.

She, smiling: You shouldn't do that.

HE: Well, I can't help it. I'm always trying to be preventive.

She: OK there, Mr. Preventive. *(She laughs, and so does he.)*

HE: I can't help it. I have learned from my mistakes.

She: OK, but we need to come up with a solution . . .

Now that he is telling her what he's worried about, which is what she wanted, she becomes more deeply engaged. Then it's his turn at humor.

HE: OK. But have you ever heard of people worried about bills? *(Smiling.)*

She, *laughing:* I've heard of those people.

HE: I am one of those people . . .

She: I'm also one of those people.

HE: . . . whether you know it or not.

She: But the thing of it is that, you know, I just pay what I can pay and the next person will have to wait. You can't give everybody money at the same time, especially when you don't have that money to give.

HE: That's true.

She: OK, but what we should do . . .

He is not done with his issue. He won't let her dismiss it so easily. He will deepen the issue and explain why he is so worried.

HE: But that's what burns me about you. We don't have that money to give, but you can go to Circuit City and buy a TV.

She: That's right. But the thing of it is that . . . OK, what should we do about this situation since bills bother you? What should we do?

HE: What do you think we should do? Pay the bills. *(Laughs.)*

She, *laughing:* That's simple. No, we should, like, have a little plan.

HE: The only thing I can do with that is have life insurance for me and you. I paid for the kids'. But now I can't pay ours.

Now he will finally tell her about the real financial jam he is in, the one he has been reluctant to discuss with her.

> **She:** Our insurance?
>
> HE: Uh-huh.
>
> **She:** So you haven't paid the insurance in a month and a half?
>
> HE: I paid the kids', but I've been trying to pay ours.
>
> **She:** You see, you don't say anything, so I be thinking that everything is OK.
>
> HE: Yeah, I gathered that, about that. *(He laughs, and so does she.)*

She is getting ready to propose a compromise.

> **She,** *getting serious:* Honestly. But what we should do is, when we get our pay-check, we need to sit down and work out how much that insurance is and how we're going to pay it.
>
> HE: Yeah.
>
> **She:** You told me that you have to pay it every three months?
>
> HE: Right.
>
> **She:** We need to figure out how we can pay that before it's due. Like maybe I can take so much out of my money, you know, and put it to the side. And since you done told me this now . . . it boils down to this: I'll just take so much out of my check.

Now she proposes a solution to the financial problem.

> HE: That's what I had planned to do, but it didn't quite work that way.
>
> **She:** Well, we'll try to figure it out, we'll try it. We'll both of us try to take something out, whatever we can come up with on the side after we get through paying everything else. We won't worry about it. We'll come up with what we can come up with.
>
> HE: Yeah, that's easy to say.

She: But when it gets toward the end to pay for it . . .

HE: Something will be there.

She: Yeah, we'll have at least something in the kitty to help pay instead of trying to come up with the money all at once.

HE: Right. That's what I'd like.

She: All right. We're whippin', baby.

This couple makes it look easy. We see them laugh and smile, yet they're serious, too. They voice their differences. But they don't punish each other. Instead, they're tolerant but beg for change, all at once. And they tiptoe toward a temporary solution. Their problems won't vanish anytime soon. They'll talk about being tight-lipped and overspending for years to come. But they're fine with that. Their problems are lifelong, but not marital death sentences.

In contrast, our gridlocked conflicts feel like fists clenched and pressed against one another. Nobody budges. Every time we confront issues that are gridlocked, the Four Horsemen appear, our feelings get trampled, and we're ready to bolt. In desperation, we think, "What's the point of working it out?"

We could be talking about finances, sex, or in-laws. It doesn't matter. We only know it goes badly. Are we just being immature? Or have we picked the wrong partner? Maybe we need some medicine. Or to tamp down being manipulative. Then again, our partner should stop competing to win and putting us down. If only we were less controlling. Or more assertive. Perhaps we're just sick, with some deep psychological disorder—a narcissistic or borderline personality disorder. Maybe we're just plain crazy. After several years of individual therapy, we could certainly vanquish this nastiness.

Thankfully, none of these theories are true. When we've studied couples who are gridlocked, we find something very different. They've tucked away a hidden dream beneath their angry words. This is stowed away for safekeeping. Then, during arguments, they only bare their teeth and sidestep the gashes of conflict. They never ask questions like "What makes this so important to you?"

Couples who have learned to dialogue about their perpetual issues ask just such questions. They ask, "Is there a story behind this
for you, maybe some childhood history that makes this so crucial
for you?" They want to uncover not just the topmost feelings, but
the deeper layers as well.

Questions like these dig up pure gold. A wife doesn't want to
just save money. She wants to avoid the crushing bankruptcy she
endured earlier. Her husband doesn't want to just spend foolishly.
He wants to travel now rather than dropping dead at fifty like his
homebound dad. Another man wants a pet dog for the kids. But
his partner is terrified of dogs. Scratch the surface? He survived the
despair of his childhood beatings by hugging the family dog. But
she was attacked at twelve by the beaten-up guard dog next door. If
no one digs beneath the surface, there's no understanding. And without understanding, there's no real dialogue or compassion. Only
fangs.

Values, dreams, and personal philosophies also underlie our gridlocked positions. We may dream of freedom or dependence. We may
long for romance or nonchalance. Money may mean our security or
our independence. Saving money may honor our family values or
transcend an ugly legacy. Special Christmas rituals may revive old
traditions or create brand-new ones. Planting a garden may connect
us to our grandmother or reconnect us to mother earth. But mean-
ness may camouflage meaning. And what we find meaningful de-
fines who we are. When we have children, these questions of legacy
become even more intensified. We are likely to want to pass down
to our children the best of our own legacy, the essence of who we
are. Is it any wonder that we can't yield on issues that are embedded with meaning for us? We're inflexible because we can't surrender the bones of who we are.

But that doesn't make dialogue impossible. Within every complaint, every hurt feeling, every blocked bid for attention, every
criticism, and every contemptuous curled lip, there is a longing.
Furthermore, within every position we have on an issue, there is
a life dream pumping blood into our being. It's not that we're

psychological disasters. We are all philosophers and visionaries. It's our values and dreams that we should be talking about. When we don't, we clash.

Our gridlocked conflicts contain the potential for great intimacy between us. But we have to feel safe enough to pull our dreams out of the closet. When we wear them, our partner may glimpse how beautiful we are—fragile but shimmering. Then, with understanding, our partners may join us in being dream catchers, rather than dream shredders.

There's always a story behind our position on an issue. But for our story to unfold, we can't encounter opposition. Nor can we think about problem solving or making compromises. Not yet. Instead, we have to focus on understanding who each of us is on this particular issue. Notice that we're not saying you need to understand just the feelings, or just the thoughts. It's beyond that. It's about also grasping what our partner holds sacred—our partner's values, beliefs, experiences, symbols, and legacies. So if we open our closed fists and extend a hand to our partner, we can let our dreams fly. But only if they won't be shot down first.

The next exercise is called the "dream within conflict exercise." It has two parts. The first part uncloaks the dreams, the stories, and the history underneath each of your positions. The second part honors each of your dreams, and will help you to reach a temporary compromise.

To help you understand Part 1, here is an abbreviated example taken from a real couple's dialogue. Their issue is housework. They will alternate being the speaker and the listener. The speaker will express his or her position on the issue, and the listener will ask questions about the dreams, values, and history beneath the speaker's viewpoint. Listen to what happens.

> **She:** Why don't you do it? Why don't you pick your clothes up? I am not your servant. I hate it when you leave them all over the floor.
>
> HE: What does this mean to you, when I leave my clothes around?

He has already made a major breakthrough just by asking this question. But will it work?

> **She:** Don't you love our home? Why do you trash it when I work so hard to build it? Don't you cherish what we have, what I am trying to build?

It doesn't work! She is so used to being defensive that it is hard for them to enter this new mode of talking about dreams.

> **HE:** What are you trying to build?
>
> **She:** To me, a home has to be neat. I can't organize my thoughts in a messy house.

Now she has told him something very important: The external disorder in the home mirrors an internal disorder she feels when the house is messy.

> **HE:** Is there some story or history behind this for you?
>
> **She:** My single mother was alcoholic. I'd come home and find her passed out and the house a total mess—dishes and dirty laundry everywhere. I vowed that when I grew up, I'd never live in a place like that. I'd have a beautiful home that was tidy and clean. Order to me means a refuge, a peaceful sanctuary where I don't have to feel alone with all the responsibility of the home on my shoulders. Disorder for me is chaos, on every level.

There is indeed a deep story to this issue for her.

> **HE:** So that's what you're trying to build? A peaceful home?
>
> **She:** Yes, that's it. A home free from chaos. OK, let's switch. You talk. What does leaving clothes around the house mean to you? Tell me the story behind your side of all this.
>
> **HE:** I'm exhausted at the end of the day, worn down. All day long I have to follow someone else's rules. A home ought to be a place where you can be free of rules, a place to unwind and be yourself.

His issue is about control, freedom, being himself at home.

> **She:** What do rules mean to you?
>
> **HE:** By telling me to pick up these few clothes I scatter around, you are making more rules for me to have to follow, trying to control me like my manager always does. You join with the enemy. I'm trying to shed my false skin, and you are not letting me do that.
>
> **She:** So for you, a home is a place to be free of rules.
>
> **HE:** Yes. But not just free. It's a place without pretensions, not a place to show others, but a place where I can be me.
>
> **She:** Free to be yourself, unbound and unfettered. Is there a history to this? Tell me the story of this.

Both dreams have now emerged, due to the safety they have created for each other.

> **HE:** My mother kept the sofas and chairs in the living room covered with plastic, and she still didn't like us kids to get on the furniture. We stayed out of the living room because it was for company. If we tracked mud into it, holy hell broke loose, so she gave us tons of rules. I had to follow the rules or she'd blow up. I hated that house.
>
> **She:** So a very neat home means it's your mother all over again?
>
> **HE:** All over again.

EXERCISE

THE DREAM WITHIN CONFLICT

Part 1: Work on a Gridlocked Issue

INSTRUCTIONS. Return to the issues you checked on the list of perpetual issues on pages 127–129. Pick one that you both think is gridlocked. Then take turns being a speaker or a listener as you discuss it. After fifteen minutes, trade roles.

If you're the speaker: It is your job to honestly describe your position on this issue. First, read the following list of sample dreams that may apply to you. Then, as you listen to your partner's questions, describe the dream that lies behind your position on this issue. What do you really want? Why is it important to you? Do you have personal history that relates to your position? Try to make your partner understand. Don't argue; just explain how you see things. Try to be as honest, open and clear as you can.

If you're the listener: You have to make your partner feel *safe* enough to tell you about the dream behind their position on the issue. It is your job to *listen*, the way a friend would listen. Only ask questions, one at a time, like the ones listed below, and listen to your partner's answers. Don't try to solve the problem. Also, don't judge your partner, or bring up your own point of view. You'll get your chance when it's your turn to speak. Instead, tell your partner that you want to hear his or her point of view and the dream and story behind it. Then, if you can, tell your partner that you support the dream and will try to make it happen in your lives.

QUESTIONS to Ask if You're the Listener

1. What does that mean to you?
2. What do you wish for or hope for? What is your dream?
3. Is there a story behind this for you?
4. Does this relate to your history in some way?
5. Tell me, why is this important to you?
6. What are all your feelings about this?
7. Are there any feelings you have left out here?
8. What do you wish for here?
9. What would be your ideal goal here?
10. What do you imagine things would be like if you got what you wanted?
11. Is there a deeper purpose or goal in this for you?
12. Does this relate to some belief or value for you?
13. Is there a fear or disaster scenario in not having this dream honored?

SAMPLE DREAMS if You're the Speaker

1. A sense of freedom
2. The experience of peace

3. Unity with nature

4. Exploring who I am

5. Adventure

6. A spiritual journey

7. Justice

8. Honor

9. Unity with my past

10. Healing

11. Knowing my family

12. Becoming all I can be

13. Having a sense of power

14. Dealing with my aging

15. Exploring a creative side of myself

16. Becoming more powerful

17. Getting over past hurts

18. Becoming more competent

19. Asking God for forgiveness

20. Exploring an old part of myself I have lost

21. Getting over a personal hang-up

22. Having a sense of order

23. Being able to be productive

24. A place and a time to just "be"

25. Being able to truly relax

26. Reflecting on my life

27. Getting my priorities in order

28. Finishing something important

29. Exploring the physical side of myself

30. Being able to compete and win

31. Travel

32. Quietness

33. Atonement

34. Building something important

35. Ending a chapter of my life

36. Saying good-bye to something

37. Love

The bottom line about dreams is this: You don't want to have the kind of relationship in which you win and are influential in the relationship but wind up crushing your partner's dreams. You want the kind of relationship in which each of you are supporting one another's dreams. If your dreams connect, so much the better.

Part 2: Honoring One Another's Dreams

You have a choice now. You can either honor your partner's position and the dream behind it, or not. That doesn't mean surrendering your own. It means trying to make peace with this issue by accepting the differences between you and establishing some kind of initial compromise on it. Compromising won't eliminate the problem. Remember, it's perpetual. So the problem will probably resurface in some other form later on. But it can transform the gridlock you've suffered into dialogue—and melt away the pain.

INSTRUCTIONS. Do this exercise in three steps. Divide your dreams into two areas.

Use the concentric-circle diagrams to do the following.

- First, define the minimal core areas that you cannot yield on.
- Second, define areas of greater flexibility that are not so hot.

Third, come up with a temporary compromise. There are different levels of honoring one another's dreams. Talk about what you can and cannot do on this issue in terms of honoring your spouse's dream *right now.* For example, you may be able to say:

I can respect your dream.

I can respect your dream and learn more about it.

I can financially support your dream to some degree.

I can join you in the dream, to some degree.

And so on. You continue from here.

Then talk about what fears each of you have about honoring your partner's dream. What "disaster scenarios" are in your mind? Then ask, how can we soothe one another's fears and reassure one another?

Now try to reach a temporary compromise by discussing the following questions: How can we support each other's dreams? How do we honor them both? What common ground do we share in our dreams? What are our common feelings, or the most important feelings here? What common goals do we have? How can these goals and dreams be accomplished? What are my areas of flexibility? Can I yield on how fast our dreams are fulfilled? or the cost, and so on? Remember:

You cannot be influential

unless you accept influence

12

SAVORING YOUR FRIENDSHIP

We had a dear friend, Bernie Zilbergeld. He worked as a sex therapist. But he should have been a comedian. Once, we were having breakfast with Bernie and his longtime girlfriend. John was dying to know how they had met. Bernie said, "Oh, she was a hooker in a hotel I was staying at." His girlfriend just rolled her eyes and smiled.

Shortly before he died, Bernie finished a study of couples' sex lives. He interviewed fifty couples who rated their sex lives as "satisfying-to-great," and fifty other couples who rated their sex lives as "not good-to-awful." Being a sex therapist, Bernie figured the satisfied group would say that their sex life was hot because they used more creative techniques than the dissatisfied group. But not so. Every one of the fifty satisfied couples exalted two priorities that had nothing to do with technicalities: (1) they made sure they stayed close friends, and (2) they simply made sex a priority. Dissatisfied couples acted like they'd never heard of these.

Picture Keith and Maria. They had their baby late; he was fifty-five, she was forty-two. They were ecstatic with their baby. Then reality set in. The baby was colicky and cried through many nights. Yet Maria was the breadwinner of the house, and needed to stay alert for her daily work. So Keith chipped in. He rose two or three times a night to bring the baby to Maria for nursing. While she worked during the day, he bottle-fed the baby the milk that Maria had breast-pumped that morning. Then came the inevitable: Maria had to go on a business trip, with Baby Michael only five weeks old! Again, Keith grabbed the reins to help out. He booked a ticket for all three of them, they traveled to Texas together, and Keith cared for Michael in the hotel while Maria worked. Exhausted but grateful, Maria would collapse into his arms every night, supported, loved, sharing her daily doings with him, and knowing that there was no better friend than Keith anywhere. He was the best.

When we have a baby, there's barely time for friendship, let alone passion and romance. We're so busy changing diapers, nursing, heating up bottles, and folding laundry, who's thinking about friendship? Yet Bernie's study tells us that we partners have to stay friends; otherwise, the fires of passion will dwindle and die. So how do we fuel our friendships when we barely have time for three words?

BUILDING AND MAINTAINING FRIENDSHIP

The transition-to-parenthood masters we studied are full of precious nuggets of wisdom. They value friendship like precious gold. And they cling to it like life itself. But they make it look easy. Here's what they do.

- *Build love maps*
- *Express appreciation, affection, and admiration*
- *Turn toward one another, not away*

Let's help you to enrich your relationships, too.

Build Love Maps.

Here's what we mean: A love map is a road map of your partner's inner psychological world. When we drive from one city to another, we've got to know how to get there. Landmarks, signs, highway numbers, bridges, even tollbooths—all become important. Without them, we are lost, and we can't get from home to our destination. Love maps are like this. We want to get from home base—that is, from ourselves—to our destination, our partner's heart. But how do we get there? By reading our partner's inner terrain. But that takes knowing who our partner is.

Do you know your partner's favorite food, his most-loved movie, his favorite relative, his most hated enemy? How about work? Do you know what your partner's passionate about in her work or what she cannot stand about it? What's the most embarrassing moment in your husband's childhood, that one time he shrunk to the floor? What's your wife's deepest-held dream, and her most cherished value?

Love maps help us feel deeply known by our partner. They also show us that our partner keenly yearns to know who we are and how we are changing over time. And what greater life-changing event is there than experiencing the birth of our child? We, ourselves, are newly reborn. Everything shifts—our values, our priorities, our dreams, even our universal attunement. So it's crucial that we turn toward our partner and ask, "And who are you now?"

How do we draw a love map of our partner's world? It's simple. The masters teach us: Just ask questions. But make them open-ended. Not ones with yes or no answers, like "Should we go to the movies tonight?" or "Did the plumber come?" Open-ended questions lead to a story. They yield bigger and deeper answers: "How do you like our apartment, now that our baby is here?" "What's your favorite part about being a father?" "What's the hardest part about being a mom?" "What's your fondest wish for our baby's childhood years?" With questions like these, we're extending an invitation: Let me visit you; tell me who you are. If we issue only statements, we're saying, "Take this," like coins of tin rather than gold as far as friendship goes. There is a little secret to good questions, though—they have to be sincere. They can't be phony. We can't ask questions just to be asking questions. We have to want to know the answers, and listen well to them. To learn more, try this next exercise.

ASK OPEN-ENDED QUESTIONS

You'll be surprised at how much your relationship will change if you shift from just making statements to asking your partner open-ended questions.

INSTRUCTIONS. First, read through the "Open-ended Questions List" that follows. Then, each of you select one question. Take turns asking your partner the question you selected, and listening to your partner's answer. If you have time, keep going and talk about another question or two. The "Open-ended Questions List" is fun to take along on a date night. Incorporate it into your conversations whenever you can.

Open-ended Questions List

How can I be a better friend to you?

How have you changed in the last year?

What do you enjoy most about being a dad (mom)?

How have your goals in life changed since our baby has come?

What are you missing most in your life since we've become parents?

What are some of your life dreams now?

What do you value the most in your life now?

Who do you think is the best parent you have ever seen? Why?

How can I be a better partner to you?

How do you think having our baby (or being pregnant) has changed our relationship?

What legacy do you want our baby to have from your family?

What are some unfulfilled dreams in your life?

What changes would you like to make in our lifestyle now that Baby has arrived?

What changes would you like to make in our home these days?

What would you like to change about our finances right now?

How has your family changed toward you since Baby arrived?

How has your outlook on life changed since you became a parent?

How are you feeling now about being a mother (father)?

What could we do to have more fun in our life?

What would you like to change about your work?

What would you like our life to be like in two years?

How would you compare yourself to your father or mother as a parent?

What kind of person would you like our baby to become?

Who does our baby remind you of in your family?

What has been your favorite time so far in our relationship?

Do you long for anything these days?

What is the biggest challenge for you as a dad (mom)?

What are your major stresses and worries these days?

What are your thoughts and feelings about religion (or spirituality) these days?

How have your political ideas changed since Baby came?

How have your friends or family changed toward you in recent years?

Express Appreciation, Affection, and Admiration

There was another gem that made our master couples shine. Every day they voiced the three As for one another: affection, appreciation, and admiration. It didn't take much. Small, everyday events evoked a word of praise or a thank-you, or a gentle touch. The gestures didn't have to be extravagant. One husband picked up the dry cleaning, and his wife said, "Hey, thanks for taking care of that." A wife made a special dessert, and her husband said, "Hmm, tastes good!" One partner cleaned out the garage, and his partner noticed and said, "Good job." "Small things often" seemed to be their motto, and it's ours as well.

So often, we look for the mistakes our partners make but neglect their contributions. We're quick to highlight their failings but not their successes. We mute our endearments but not our criticisms. And the days that pass without kindness mount up, until we no longer know whether we're viewed as lovers or liabilities. We have to change our habit of mind. We have to stop scanning the environment for our husband's mistakes and telescope in on his achievements. And there are many. Likewise, we can't focus on what our wife hasn't done; we have to appreciate what she has done. And that's plenty. With a new baby, there's never enough time to do it all. So we have to be thankful for what our partners manage to do, despite being exhausted and overwhelmed. But having admiring and appreciative thoughts isn't enough; the thoughts have to come out of our mouths or be conveyed with our touch.

The moral to the story is this: Catch your partner doing something right, and say, "Thanks," "Good job," or "You're terrific." And one way or another, say, "I love you," as often as you can. That's most important of all.

EXERCISE

EXPRESS APPRECIATION

INSTRUCTIONS. In this next exercise, read over the list of your partner's positive qualities. Choose three items from the list that you appreciate about your partner. Then, for each item, think of a time when your partner demonstrated that particular quality. Jot down a note about it next to the item. Now share with your partner the items you chose, and your memories of them in your partner. If you wish, you can also choose more than three items. But don't punish your partner for only coming up with three to begin with. Remember, it may be a new habit you are developing here, and it takes time for new habits to take hold.

Your Partner's Positive Qualities

Your partner's energy

Your partner's strength

Your partner's ability to take charge

Your partner's flexibility

Your partner's sensitivity

How well your partner listens to you

How well your partner supports you

How well your partner responds to your moods

Your partner's warmth

Your partner's enthusiasm

Your partner's ability to have fun

Your partner's ability as a lover

Your partner's sensuality

Your partner as a refuge for you

Your partner's dependability

Your partner's tenderness

Your partner's imagination

Your partner's creativity

Your partner's artistry

Your partner's eyes

Your partner's trustworthiness

Your partner's passion

Your partner's romantic nature

Your partner's gracefulness

Your partner's compassion

Your partner's amiability

Your partner's hospitality

The way your partner kisses you

Your partner's playfulness

Your partner's ability to be a good friend to others

Your partner's competence

Your partner's parenting of your baby

Your partner's sense of humor

Your partner's looks in clothes

Your partner's looks without clothes

Your partner's loyalty

Your partner's sense of style

Your partner's values

Your partner's sense of morality

Your partner's social activism

Your partner's spirituality

Other:

Turn Toward One Another, Not Away

Our transition masters had one more jewel tucked away in their bag of tricks. At first, as we watched hundreds of hours of their videotaped time together, we couldn't figure out what they were doing that was making such a big difference in the quality of their relationship. And we were bored silly. But then we noticed: Nearly every time one partner made a bid for attention, the other partner responded to it. It could be as simple as this.

"Hey, honey, look at that pretty boat out there."

"Wow!"

We realized that every bid for attention constituted a need, small or big. It might be verbal or nonverbal. "Please pass the butter" was obvious. But "Did you read this article in the paper?" wasn't. If the partner responded with "OK, here's the butter" in the first case, or with silence or, worse yet, "Stop bugging me. I'm trying to read," in the second, two different outcomes emerged later. In the first, relationships succeeded; in the second, they were more likely to fail.

What's the difference? In the first case, one partner turned toward his spouse and responded to the other's request; in the second case, the partner turned away from her spouse's bid for attention or, worse, turned against her partner with irritability.

Bids for attention are really bids for emotional connection. For example, when our partner calls out our name, how do we respond? We can either say, "Yes?" with some sweetness (turning toward), say nothing (turning away), or "What do you want now?" with annoyance (turning against). Depending on how we respond, we'll either be making a deposit in our relationship bank account when we turn toward, or losing some assets (turning away or turning against). Or worse, we might even be going into the red. Once our bid is refused, we crumple a little, and we're unlikely to make a bid again. Then we're headed for trouble. But if we respond positively, or, even better, with enthusiasm, we'll be deep in the black and cruising.

So all those little moments when our partners are stating their needs or reaching out for attention turn out to be incredibly important in sustaining our friendships. And how we respond means nearly everything. Granted, we won't respond perfectly every time. We're only human, after all. But we don't need to have high standards to start a new process of bidding and turning toward. We just need increased awareness of how our partner expresses his or her needs.

Here's a law we discovered in our lab: Turning toward leads to more turning toward. So we can start small. For, as the Scots jokingly say, "Many a little makes a lottle." And the more we turn toward our partner with graciousness, the stronger and more long-lasting our friendship will be. All those moments of turning toward each other in the smallest moments are relationship investments, and they're worth their weight in gold.

TURNING TOWARD YOUR PARTNER'S NEEDS

INSTRUCTIONS. Read the list that follows, and select a need that you have from it. Then take turns. Each of you, describe the need you selected to your partner. Try to be as specific about it as you can. If you're the listener, ask your partner for suggestions about how you can meet this need better in the coming week. You can refer to this list from time to time later on to help you voice your needs to your partner. Just remember, do your best to turn toward your partner, not away or against him or her.

Needs List for Turning Toward

- I need you to be more physically affectionate.
- I need to cuddle more.
- I need to talk more about the baby.
- I need you to answer me when I call your name.
- I need you to ask me about my hopes.
- I need to talk every day about how my day went and to hear about your day.
- I need more help with housework.
- I need to get some time alone.
- I need for us to go on a date sometime.
- I need the TV to be on less often.
- I need a foot rub or a back rub.
- I need to invite some friends over.
- I want us to divide up the chores.
- I need you and me to do more things as a family.
- I want to order food in or have you do the cooking one night.
- I want you to run my bath water and let me take a long bath.
- I need to see my friends.
- I want us to spend more time with my parents.

154

- I need an adventure.
- I need you to tell me that I look nice.
- I need a kiss hello and a kiss good-bye every day.
- I need you to play with the baby.
- I need to travel.

FRIENDSHIP AND CONSTRUCTIVE CONFLICT

These three parts of friendship (love maps, fondness and admiration, and turning toward) affect the way people are when they disagree. They actually have a lot more access to their sense of humor, to their affection, to all the positive things, the positive energies that really make it possible to have constructive disagreements or to live with them in a much more constructive and creative way. This is all about earning and building up what we call "points." You want lots of points built up in your relationship. Otherwise, you will be living at the bone, or your gas tank will be running on empty. These three levels of the sound relationship house are fundamental because through them you are able to have access to positive emotions during times of disagreement. That's what the masters do. They can laugh at themselves, and they can be understanding toward their partners, even when they disagree.

FRIENDSHIP AND ROMANCE, PASSION, AND GREAT SEX

The other thing we discovered that was very surprising is that these three parts of friendship are the basis for romance, passion, and good sex (we really didn't expect this). It could be said that every positive thing you do in a relationship is actually a form of foreplay. And that's where we began in this chapter—talking about sex.

13

HEAT UP YOUR SEX LIFE

Let's talk about sex. You may think that a lot is known about a couple's sex life and how to keep it alive. Not true. Most sex-advice books for couples are full of fantasy. The wrong fantasy, that is, one that assumes that couples are the same before they have kids and after. Let's find out the real story—one straight from our lab.

Sara said that soon after the baby arrived, she returned to work. At noon every day, she dashed to the restroom and pumped milk. Later, she rushed home to breast-feed the baby. Her breasts hurt all the time, and she grew exhausted. And she was always angry at Jim, her husband. *He* didn't have to rush home from work. *He* didn't hurt. They were no longer playing on a level field. Meanwhile, she continued to "pleasure" Jim. That was fine, but she wasn't at all turned on. In fact, her desire had cooled down to dry ice, while Jim's stayed hot. Sara was very upset by these changes in their romantic life. She decided that she and Jim should get some advice from the experts.

So Sara went to Barnes & Noble and scanned books for over three hours. She sent Jim to gather information on his own.

Jim went to a bookstore. He quickly found a book about how much fun sex can be. He salivated over the drawings of new sexual positions. He thought Sara would love this book. After buying it, he pursued one of its recommendations. He bought whipped cream— ten cans of it. He proudly returned home, cans in hand.

157

Meanwhile, Sara stood in the sex section of the bookstore, thumbing through volume after volume. Nothing seemed right. No book fit how she felt.

Sara's anxiety escalated. Maybe something was wrong with her. She pondered: "Maybe I'm not like other women. I'm certainly not like the ones in these books. I have no interest in sex with Jim—or any man, for that matter. Maybe I've become a lesbian. Could that be?" She left empty-handed. But remembering one book she had tossed aside, she stopped at a drugstore to buy an over-the-counter lubricant. The label on the tube advised women not to use this product if they were pregnant or breast-feeding. Disgusted, she replaced it on the shelf and returned to her car.

When Sara got home, she was totally fed up and depressed. Jim's excitement, however, was palpable. He showed her his new book, his favorite drawings, and the cans of whipped cream. Sara snorted with disdain. Instead of making love that night, they fought like tigers. Jim felt devastated. Sara felt drowned in despair. They slunk off to separate rooms.

Later that evening, after the baby fell asleep, they tiptoed back to the living room to talk. Sara cried with Jim. She confessed that she felt like a freak. She wanted to feel sexual, but just couldn't. Jim listened. He was worried, but he held her affectionately and reassured her that he'd be patient and affectionate. Sarah sighed with gratitude.

The next week, they met with their family doctor. Sara told him about her feelings, and he prescribed Prozac for her. She drove right to the pharmacy, downed her first pill in the parking lot, and took it daily from then on. But several weeks later, Sara's sexual desire had plummeted from ground level to the basement. She and Jim stopped touching altogether.

Another few months passed. Sara stopped breast-feeding. Like a new spring, Sara's sexual desire slowly bubbled up again. Hesitantly, Sara told Jim about it. He was astonished. She exclaimed that it must have been the breast-feeding that wiped out her libido. "Makes total sense," said Jim. Sara screwed up her courage to talk to a few older women she knew. One after another, they confirmed her story. Sara wondered, "Why didn't I find a book that says how many breast-feeding women lose their desire for sex, that said it's totally natural? Then I would have realized I wasn't abnormal. Someone should write that book." She's right.

Nowadays Jim and Sara's sex life is back on track. Maybe even better. Jim is glad he listened to Sara instead of shutting down like he wanted to. These days, sex isn't as frequent as Jim would like, but it's no longer at zero. And now those whipped cream cans have all been emptied, some in the bedroom.

In short, most books out there are not grounded in studies of what real couples face. And none ask questions like these: What happens to intimacy after a baby arrives? And what actually works for couples? We wanted answers to questions like these, so we could help couples like Jim and Sara. So together with Julia Heiman from the Kinsey Institute for Research in Sex, Gender, and Reproduction, we studied couples on their journey into parenthood.

First, we examined our legacy of knowledge. There were some great sex researchers like Alfred Kinsey, and John Masters and Virginia Johnson, but they hadn't studied couples. Masters and Johnson's classic books on sex written in the 1970s were based on studying individuals masturbating. We realized we had to start from the beginning. We asked, how are couples' sex lives related to how they talk to each other at the end of a day? Related to how they eat dinner together? Connected to how they cuddle, or compliment one another, or exchange affection? And to how they conflict?

We talked to couples three years after their babies' births. What had worked and not worked in their sex lives after their babies arrived years ago? And in the past four weeks, how much did they feel sexual desire or interest? Here's what we discovered. On average, three years after the blessed event, women reported feeling desire about once a *week*, while men said they felt desire about once a *day*. Women wanted to be touched sexually, on average, once every two weeks, while men hungered for it two to three times a week.

When we asked about experiencing orgasm during sexual activity, men reported climaxing six times more often than women! Again, this is three years postbaby. Then when we asked them to rate how sexual they felt (on a 5-point scale), women rated themselves a meager 2.95 (not very), while men rated themselves 4.25 (extremely).

We also asked our couples to reflect on their sex lives before Baby. For times of courtship and pregnancy, men's and women's ratings mirrored each other and appeared to be good to great. But between then and the time of our survey, three years after the baby, it looked like the stork in the sky had dropped its bundle, but crushed their sex lives. Having a baby was no aphrodisiac, at least not to the women.

But just to be sure, we scrutinized other data from our lab. In earlier research, we had studied young couples longitudinally, following them from wedding through their next ten years to evaluate their relationship quality. Some of these couples had had babies along the way. We compared the couples who had just had a baby to the couples who remained childless. The couples were matched on how long they had been married and how happy they were with their relationships. Did having a baby cool down couples' desire, passion, and good sex? Yes, indeed. With no Baby, the fires burned bright. But with Baby came buckets of cold water. Afterward, steam remained, but no more flames. Taken together, the studies confirm our theory. Many couples sexually disconnect after Baby is born, and that gap may last for as long as three years! Before Baby, most everybody wants sex. After Baby, men want sex a lot more than women.

Certainly, biology takes a toll. After giving birth, some women's hormones take a tumble. Libido vanishes down the rabbit hole, especially with nursing. But sexual feelings mirror relationship satisfaction, too. When closeness dwindles, sexual desire evaporates.

Of course, there are exceptions to these patterns. Not all couples are the same. Among some postbaby couples, wives yearned more for sex than their husbands. Other couples happily exclaimed that after Baby, their sex lives blossomed. But, unfortunately, these couples weren't the majority.

To learn more, we got nosier, and couples were only too happy to talk. We asked them if they'd share the details of their sex lives. To ensure their comfort, we interviewed partners separately, where they could maintain confidentiality, even from one another. We were dying to know: What were the secrets of the successful couples?

The answers were fascinating. Our master couples resurrected their diminished sex lives through affectionate *nonsexual* touching. In other words, they continued touching one another even in those months when their sexual desire was low. Women love their partner's physical affection, provided their partners are genuine about it. They don't resent it.

And what makes men glow? To see that gleam in their wives' eyes that reads, "Husband, you are gorgeous." In other words, after-baby sex is exquisite when men feel desired and wanted by their women. Who knew that feeling attractive was as important to men as to women? Women transmit their desire through nonsexual touch and affection or golden compliments on how handsome their men look. As one husband mentioned, "I can take not having sex for a while, as long I know that I am still wanted. That's it for me. That's the bottom line." In other words, *all positive interactions are foreplay.*

Here's what we mean. When your partner looks tired, and you do the dishes even when it's not your turn, that's foreplay. When you tell your partner how good he or she looks to you (even after being up all night with Baby), that's foreplay. When you take care of the baby so your partner can have some time alone, that's foreplay. When you listen to one another after a stressful day, that's also foreplay. When you take a walk together in the morning and talk to each other, when you say thank you even when you don't have to, and when you sincerely tell your partner how beautiful or handsome she or he looks, that's all foreplay. So, are you enjoying foreplay? Or just expecting fireworks without a lit fuse?

Let's begin with a self-test to evaluate your sexual relationship. We know this might seem scary, but have faith; we can help you to make positive changes if you want them, too.

SELF-TEST: HOW'S YOUR SEX LIFE?

Fill out this questionnaire separately and compare answers later, after you have scored your own. Each of you, read the items we have listed to indicate if this area is fine or if it needs improvement. Put an check mark in every box that you think applies to your relationship now.

	NOT A PROBLEM	A PROBLEM
1. We are emotionally close.	___	___
Just simply talking to each other is . . .	___	___
Staying emotionally in touch is . . .	___	___
Feeling taken for granted is. . .	___	___
My partner knowing me well is . . .	___	___
My partner being emotionally disengaged is . . .	___	___
Spending time together is . . .	___	___
My being emotionally disengaged is . . .	___	___

	NOT A PROBLEM	A PROBLEM
2. The relationship is romantic and passionate.	___	___
My partner being verbally affectionate is . . .	___	___
My partner's expressing love often enough is . . .	___	___
Our touching each other enough is . . .	___	___

Our feeling very romantic is . . .   ___   ___

Our cuddling enough is . . .   ___   ___

My partner wanting to massage me is . . .   ___   ___

Our having tender moments is . . .   ___   ___

Our having passionate moments is . . .   ___   ___

My feeling attractive to my partner is . . .   ___   ___

My finding my partner attractive is . . .   ___   ___

                                                    NOT A PROBLEM   A PROBLEM

3. Our sex life is . . .   ___   ___

Wanting more sex than my partner is . . .   ___   ___

My partner wanting more sex than me is . . .   ___   ___

My not being satisfied with sex is . . .   ___   ___

My partner being OK with my
masturbating is . . .   ___   ___

My not being OK with my partner's
masturbating is   ___   ___

My partner not being satisfied with sex is . . .   ___   ___

Being able to talk about sexual problems is . . .   ___   ___

My often feeling rejected sexually is . . .   ___   ___

My partner feeling rejected sexually is . . .   ___   ___

My need for more adventure in sex is . . .   ___   ___

My partner being bored with our sex life is . . .   ___   ___

Being able to talk about sex at all is . . .   ___   ___

Our wanting different things sexually is . . .   ____   ____

My rarely having orgasms is . . .   ____   ____

My partner rarely having orgasms is . . .   ____   ____

My having problems with desire is . . .   ____   ____

My partner having problems with desire is . . .   ____   ____

Not enough love in our lovemaking is . . .   ____   ____

My partner thinking there isn't enough love
in our lovemaking is . . .   ____   ____

For your score, add up all the times you checked that an area was a problem. If your score *or* your partner's score is greater than or equal to 10, then you need to work on improving your sex life.

Here's how. Our master couples share ten secrets for having great sex after Baby.

SECRETS OF COUPLES WHOSE SEX LIFE IS GOING WELL

1. *Accept that things have changed since the baby arrived.*

2. *Ask each other for sex.*

3. *Talk about what feels good sexually, and how to make it better.*

4. *Continue nonsexual affection, especially touch.*

5. *Realize that in most cases, he's a microwave and she's a Dutch oven.*

6. *Accept that quickies are as important as gourmet sex.*

7. *Accept masturbation to orgasm, and continue to have oral sex (if you've always liked it).*

8. *Share your sexual fantasies.*

9. *Discuss your innermost feelings and don't avoid conflict.*

10. *Prioritize gourmet sex and make time for it.*

We'll explain each secret so you, too can heat up your relationship with passion.

1. Accept That Things Have Changed Since the Baby Arrived

Our couples who have mastered the transition to parenthood accept that the rules are new now that Baby has arrived. They aren't thrilled, but they hang in there. They don't fault the relationship. They know we're all mired in the same mud, and they carve out new pathways to link up to each other. They become a better team. They commiserate and they celebrate—together.

Most women gain weight during pregnancy, so they feel unattractive after childbirth. The humorist David Barry said that when your wife asks you if she looks fat in this dress, the only thing you can possibly do is to fall on the floor and pretend you're having a heart attack. Any other response and you're in trouble. Our data on postbaby couples agree! Husbands must hush up their comments on weight gain. That means avoid suggestions that she work out, eat differently, dress differently, and be in any way more like you . . . on pain of marital death! Instead, be understanding, gentle, and patient. Be affectionate and appreciative of what you *do* find attractive. Remember, all appreciations are foreplay.

2. Ask Each Other for Sex

In most cultures in the United States, heterosexual couples typically are indirect about amorous feelings. We send out little probes to scout out if our partner is in the mood. So a fellow whispers, "Is it a little cold in here, sweetie?" His gal might say, "You betcha. Come over here, big boy." Then he's in business. But what if she clips out, "Nope. Not at all." Then he can mutter, "Oh. Guess I'll put on a sweater." Good, he's saved face. No, this wasn't really a sexual overture. But what if he opens up with "Would you like to make love?" and he gets "No"? It's like she's sneering, "Make love to you? No way. I'd rather walk the dog." Sound familiar? So if we don't want to send out feelers, we end up not asking at all.

Our study of gay and lesbian couples and our *Reader's Digest* survey of Latino-American couples opened our eyes to another way. Being more open and direct about sex can really pay off. Both of these groups speak their minds about sex. Sex isn't a hot potato for them; it's more like a slice of bread. So when raising the topic, they're less embarrassed and defensive. As a result, both groups know better what their partners prefer. Above all, both groups seem sexually happier, even after kids. In fact, Latino men feel more masculine when they know their partners' sexual wishes and satisfy them. No wonder Don Juan was such a success.

We don't necessarily advocate total directness for everyone. Many of us come by our Puritan restraint honestly. But experimenting at the edges of our comfort zone will probably do no harm and may do heaps of good.

Sometimes we may be sexually mismatched with our partner in the desire department. We knew one couple in which the woman wanted sex three times a day, despite just having had a baby, and the man wanted intimacy once a week—that was plenty! Though their gender roles are actually reversed in most cases, the problem remains the same: a desire mismatch. This may be a time for compromise. We may not be in the mood, but with some stimulation, we can get there. Or we can offer intimacy to our partners as a gift, like a delicious dessert. In the 1960s, books for couples used to recommend that wives greet their husbands' return by sheathing themselves in nothing but Saran Wrap (not so great for skin ducts). We don't have to go that far! On the other hand, we women go out of our way to buy flowers or bake a cake; why not don the negligee, lie back, and enjoy our partner's glee? Male partners can also offer a massage, and then ask if it's OK to advance to intimacy. But every partner must also have the right to say no and have that answer respected. Sex should never be forced or foisted on a partner if it's not wanted. Respecting our partner's boundaries must come first. And when there's respect, softening may come later.

So we suggest trying to be more direct. Agree with one another that you will ask for sex when you're in the mood. And agree on a way to refuse when you're not. For instance, try using a 9-point scale of amorous feelings, with 1 representing "Not at all in the mood," and 9 representing "Yes, very much in the mood." Then one of you can say, "Honey, the kids are asleep and tonight I'm a 7. How about you?" The reply might be a gentle "No, sorry, I'm a 2 tonight." Or, "I'm a 5; convince me." Or, if you're lucky, "I think I have been a 9 all day. Let's go!"

3. Talk About What Feels Good Sexually, and How to Make It Better

Many of us would choose to discuss laxatives over lovemaking any day. Here, our master couples have great advice for us. They follow four ground rules.

1. *Agree to be honest, but very gentle with each other.*

2. *Only say what you do like in bed, not what you don't like.*

3. *Compliment one another and reminisce about the good times you have had in bed with one another.*

4. *Keep an open mind, and know that in time you will become better lovers if you just keep the talk lines open about sex.*

In one of our workshops, one couple had stopped talking to one another. We stepped in and asked them what had silenced them. This burly, handsome man said that he was offended. "I make love a certain way. It's my way. If she doesn't like it, too bad. There's my way, or the highway." We then asked him, on another topic, how he would learn to give a good massage to his partner. Quick as a cat, he replied, "I'd just ask her what felt good and what didn't." Ah-hah. We told him lots of people felt the way he did. Feedback about our lovemaking can feel like a personal rejection. But not when we know our partner wants more intimacy with us. So it's great to share with our partners what we want sexually, including what kind of touch, where to touch, whether or not we want oral sex, what position we prefer, and so on. Fulfilling our partner's wishes paves the way for our paths to merge—lovingly.

4. Express Nonsexual Affection, Especially with Touch

Whether man or woman, we all need nonsexual affection, not just sex. Touch helps us feel more desirable, more cherished, and more intimate emotionally. With touch we know we're allies, not adversaries.

In the United States, however, we treat touch like our portal to the plague. A psychologist named Sidney Jourard observed couples dining out in several cities, and he counted how many times they simply touched each another in an hour. The average was 115 times in Paris, and 185 times in Mexico City. But in London it was zero, and in Gainesville, Florida, 2!

In this country, nobody gets touched much, not even our children. And in recent years, it's only gotten worse after the sexual-abuse scandals in our schools and churches. Now teachers and teacher's aides are advised not to touch children, even when young ones are physically hurt and needing comfort.

Psychologist Tiffany Field of the University of Miami set up a "do-touch" nursery school. Parents know that in her school, their children will be physically comforted if they fall down. Video cameras in the school ensure that there is no unwanted or inappropriate touch. There, Field did an experiment. She compared sixty means of physically comforting children with sixty methods of verbally comforting them. She found fifty-three physical methods to be effective, compared with only three of the verbal methods. No wonder kids feel loved and safe there.

Field has also conducted over ninety-five studies in her "touch research centers" throughout the world. The effects of touch are astounding, especially with premature babies. Unlike those who receive standard medical care, preemies who are massaged fifteen minutes a day increase their weight, on average, 47 percent in ten days! Not that we postbaby wives would want the same. But Fields also found that postpartum mothers benefit from daily massage; the effects are comparable to those of antidepressant medications. And no sideways drops in libido like poor Sara suffered (the woman we mentioned at the beginning of this chapter). Massage also adds the benefit of husbands massaging their wives, so partners really do stay "in touch."

In sum, we can go a long a way toward staving off depression and keeping our sexual fire stoked by giving each other a fifteen-minute deep massage every day. It feels great!

5. Realize That in Most Cases, He's a Microwave and She's a Dutch Oven

There's no perfect way to have sex. But here's a story we hear over and over again. For women, sex is a slow buildup, and for men, it's a quick release. Men turn toward woman for sex once they're aroused and erect. But she's got more laundry to fold before she can even get to bed. Ever experienced that?

Sex works best after Baby's arrival when men slow way down,

talk first, caress their women slowly, and let them know how much they are loved and seen as beautiful. It also doesn't hurt for women to tell their men that they're gorgeous, too. Then you're cookin'.

6. Accept That Quickies Are as Important as Gourmet Sex

Couples happy with their sex life know the facts: Babies seem to have a radar for parental lovemaking and always need something at exactly the wrong time. So sometimes, sex had better be quick, as in better fireworks than fizzles. Happy couples find surefire ways for her to climax, like oral or manual clitoral stimulation, and sometimes his just having the orgasm is fine, too. Some women say that they like offering their partners "a sexual gift." In other words, couples find ways to feel close even during less-romantic and non-gourmet sexual encounters. Remember, what provides the spark for quickies is verbal and physical affection.

7. Accept Masturbation to Orgasm, and Continue to Have Oral Sex (If You've Always Liked It)

The famous Sex in America study by Edward Laumann, Robert Michael, and Gina Kolata, reported that married and cohabiting people have more sex than single people. Married men in particular have more, even with themselves. So the truth is . . . married men masturbate. Surprised? Masturbation especially comes in handy when babies arrive. It's a perfectly normal way of coping with sexual needs that doesn't take sexuality outside family bounds. And it may preserve the health of the couple relationship.

In our study, couples whose sex lives were doing well after the baby's arrival embraced all kinds of sexual experience, including masturbation alone or together. But if masturbation wasn't discussed or accepted, couples' sex lives backfired. Here's an example.

James and Brenda had a baby. They were so busy they forgot to talk, for months. One day, Brenda walked in on James masturbating to Internet pornography. What a betrayal! She was devastated. She cried to him that his masturbating to pictures of nude women was a statement that she was ugly, they were beautiful, and he no longer found her attractive. Chastened, James nodded in apology. But secretly, he didn't get it. To avoid more conflict with Brenda, he said he'd forgo the pornography. But to himself, he vowed to just be more discreet. Inevitably, a few months later he got caught again. This time, Brenda screamed that the relationship was over; James had shattered her trust and their relationship.

The story of James and Brenda, unfortunately, underscores a crucial point: In committed relationships, sex is personal. Unless pornography is accepted by both partners, it can feel like non-monogamy—in other words, a profound betrayal. And after Baby arrives, the betrayal feels even more intense.

Brenda helped us understand this in our interview with her. She was a very attractive woman, and she was used to men lustfully staring at her and whistling. But since she'd become a mother, the catcalls had stopped.

Recently, she'd been walking alone at a shopping mall. She happened to have on a red clingy, low-cut dress. She figured she looked great. There were three young men sitting around a fountain. She swung by them, but there was nary a look, let alone a whistle. She was stunned and chagrined. At home, she immediately shed her clothes and studied herself in a full-length mirror. "That's strange," she thought. "I am more buff now than before the baby. Why don't they look at me anymore?"

But as our interviewer asked her more questions, Brenda admitted that at the moment she walked by those three men, her mind was filled with thoughts of errands and to-do lists. She was "Mom-on-a-mission," getting things done. She also confessed that at that moment, she was angry at James, "as always . . ." She added laughingly, "Probably these thoughts of mine didn't transmit a very sexy image to these guys."

Brenda was right. Women's sexuality takes a dip psychologically and biologically when Baby arrives. Moms are preoccupied with the survival of their baby. Though nurturant, they're also fiercely protective of their young, like she-bears who fend off dangerous predators three times the size of their cubs. Nurturant and fierce doesn't usually read as sexy and attractive. So men, of course, will respond differently.

But Brenda's dilemma wasn't just biologically driven. James had a hand in Brenda's feeling unattractive and angry, too. He was quite passive in their relationship. He hardly ever initiated sex. And when Brenda did, he often said no. Worst of all, he never romanced Brenda. So, once she stopped acting seductively, sexual energy drained out of their relationship. Then up came her anger. The sad truth was that Brenda needed James to romance her more than she ever had before. But what happened instead? James turned to Internet porn. No wonder Brenda was shattered.

In contrast, how do successful couples manage differences in their desire for sex and romance? Mary and David are a great example. Mary said that when she married, she had a lot to learn about men and masturbation. Her sheltered and religious upbringing had predisposed her against it. At first, David's talking about masturbation disturbed her. But they kept on talking about it. She asked him lots of questions, and turned to her experienced girlfriends to understand more about normal sexual development. After a time, she changed her mind. She understood that David's masturbation was normal and healthy and not something sick or nasty. She could support it as an alternative when she was too sleepy or stressed for intimacy.

These days, Mary also enjoys giving oral sex to David. And she has learned to ask for it for herself, too. David finds that very sexy. Mary also gives David a hand in climaxing.

Not all successful couples are like Mary and David. Some women tolerate their man's masturbation, but prefer not to help them along. In other couples, women find masturbation fun when their men aren't in the mood, but their men prefer not to masturbate. In still others, couples choose to manually stimulate each other.

The key point here is that if we can stay open to alternative forms of sexual fulfillment, our sex lives can simmer along until we're ready to resume full intercourse again. Above all, we need to share our frustrations and needs, and lovingly honor our partner's wishes.

8. Share Your Sexual Fantasies

Will and Betty had a favorite fantasy. They'd drive across town to their favorite nightclub, then separate when they got there. He'd be the tall, sexy stranger in the fedora. She'd be the blond dame at the bar. He'd sidle up to her and ask her name. She'd huskily reply. They were off and running. They'd move through the fantasy of strangers meeting, seductively entrancing each other, and slow-dancing right into the "bedroom." Which was, of course, in their own house.

Jake and Lilly would play boss and secretary. He'd perch his glasses down his nose and sit busily writing at his desk. She'd swish into the room in her tight tank top and shortest skirt. They wouldn't leave the home office for hours.

Couples who keep their sex lives burning have rich and imaginative sexual fantasies that they talk about and live out. Now, all of us have special images and wishes; they form the landscape of our inner erotic world. But Baby's arrival may flood our old erotic roadways. Do we know how to find each other then? Here's the lesson: We have to keep talking about our fantasies. If we do, we'll traverse our sexual landscape together, even as it shifts and changes.

As you can imagine, opening up our erotic inner lives takes courage and trust. Many of us have been shamed for even having fantasies. So trusting our partners with our sexual fantasies takes time. It helps to start small and try mild things first.

In general, men's fantasies tend to be more visual and brief. Women's fantasies tend to be longer with more narrative and emotional content. Fantasies may include stories of seduction by teachers, journalists, athletes, actors, pastors, partygoers, kings, animals, cavemen—you name it. Costumes may get crazy. Imagery may involve control, no control, and everything in between. A man orders his partner to do things she finds erotic, or she does likewise to him. Taboo-breaking fantasies are common, too, like having sex in Grand Central Station, or imagining having more than one partner. Some couples also fuel their fantasies with written or visual pornography, and most do lots of talking, whatever their fantasy. All of it is fine, and normal.

We think Mark and Marge sum it up best. "She knows my fantasies now, and she never did before. And now I know hers. It's way cool. Best of all, she teaches me about the holiness of sex, the healthiness of it." We agree.

9. Discuss Your Innermost Feelings and Don't Avoid Conflict

It's difficult to talk about our inner life when we know we'll end up in battle. Couples in our study tell us that the hardest thing to share with one another is their attraction to someone else. The late psychologist Shirley Glass had some very deep insights to share with us about why this is so. She worked with couples who'd suffered infidelity. Her greatest gift was taking infidelity out of the pulpit, making it seem less like a sick and immoral sin, and more like the sad but natural consequence of marital loneliness. She heard many stories like the following.

Harry was feeling exhausted, neglected, lonely, and horny. One day, he had a very interesting conversation at an office party with one of his coworkers, Helen. He and Helen laughed together, told one another their life stories, and commiserated about their tyrant of a boss. After a second glass of wine, Harry also complained about how difficult life had been since the baby had arrived. Liz, his wife, was now so absorbed with their baby that there was no time for him anymore. Helen was very understanding. She whispered reassurances. Harry felt much better. Nothing physical happened between Harry and Helen. There was no touching or hand-holding or kissing. But afterward, Harry found himself thinking of Helen, not Liz.

While driving home, Harry thought, "Liz and I haven't had that kind of fun together in a long time. I should go home and tell Liz about my conversation with Helen. I should tell her that I am worried—we never talk like that anymore." But then Harry imagined Liz's reaction. He knew she'd be furious and upset. Liz would call Harry a big baby. She would tell him to grow up. She would tell him that's it's no picnic for her either, and he should shape up. Then he would feel guilty and awful. So he thought, "The heck with it, I just won't say anything. Nothing really happened anyway. What she doesn't know won't hurt her. Or me."

But then Harry had a secret. He didn't tell Liz about Helen. And he was now protecting his friendship with Helen.

Relationships are built with walls and windows, Dr. Glass tells us. The walls partners erect around their relationships keep others out and privacy in, while the windows stay open between them. But that changed for Harry and Liz. Now Helen had a window into Harry and Liz's inner sanctum, but there was a wall shutting Liz out from Harry and Helen's new friendship. A marital transgression had occurred. Not a big one, but one just the same.

Harry avoided Liz because he felt bad about keeping a secret from her. He grew more withdrawn, but lonelier, too. So the next time Harry and Helen talked, Harry hungered to open up again to Helen. This time, Harry gave himself permission to gaze into Helen's eyes. She was beautiful. He touched her hand. He felt a zing. That scared him. He mumbled something and scurried back to his desk. This time he definitely wouldn't tell Liz what happened.

There were more "chance" encounters, then coffees, lunches, after-office-hour drinks, and, finally, motels. It all happened slowly, but surely. Harry had no intentions at the start, not even in the middle. He just knew that he was lonely, and that he was afraid to share his secrets, and those secrets eventually grabbed hold of him and took him for a ride. It could happen to anyone.

The mistake Harry made was not discussing his feelings with Liz right from the start. Gradually, emotional distance between them grew and their intimacy dwindled. And Harry gave himself permission to cross boundaries.

Loneliness opens up cracks in relationships, leaving relationships vulnerable to the protective walls of Jericho tumbling down. Over the rubble can step the "other," and an affair can follow. In actuality, Harry wasn't an evil person. Liz wasn't a bad partner. And Helen wasn't a home wrecker. The problem was that when potential conflict loomed, Harry ducked for cover and stopped talking. And Liz asked no questions.

Only by understanding this process can we learn how to prevent an affair from happening in the first place, and heal from it if it already has.

Most affairs are not about sex. They are about finding someone to talk to who listens to us, laughs at our jokes, and finds us fascinating. And, once again, biology takes a front-row seat. When we affiliate and feel close to someone, particularly a potential sexual partner, the hormones oxytocin and vasopressin get secreted by the pituitary gland in our brain. Men secrete these specific hormones when they make friends or become closer to another man; women secrete them when they lactate, make friends, or become closer to another woman. These hormones lubricate emotional bonding. So when Harry let himself get closer to Helen, even innocently, his hormones paved the way toward their bonding.

Over the years, we have treated many couples who are recovering from an affair. People often tell themselves that no one will be hurt as long as the affair remains a secret. What spouses don't know can't hurt them. But we have learned that even if an affair remains secret, the person *carrying the secret* is hurt. The secret-carrier isn't free to be close to his or her spouse. Intimacy is irrevocably damaged, and she or he loses a helpmate. Unless they can talk about what happened, no repairs are possible. And if the secret is discovered, the injuries to trust, friendship, and intimacy infect every inch of the relationship for everyone, parents and children both. An affair is like gangrene. Without amputating the affair partner from the relationship, then cleaning the remaining wound, strengthening the body that remains, and learning to live with the scars, healing is impossible, and marital demise is likely.

Recovering from an affair involves a willingness to talk even when it's most difficult, to answer questions, and to eventually transcend the trauma of betrayal. Here's the story of a couple who healed, unlike Harry and Liz.

Bob was a cop with a local police force. Powerfully built inside and out and good at his job, he was in line for a detective's badge. A gentle husband and father, he was also finishing a college degree at night. Lonnie, his wife, worked in the local unemployment office. After the baby, they were very busy but remained good friends.

But it was hard for Bob to talk about work. Once he went home from the gory scene of a traffic accident in which an entire family was killed. When Lonnie asked him about his day, he casually noted, "Oh, boring as usual." He didn't want her troubled by the bloody images he had seen that day. That night, his dreams were strewn with bodies. He awakened screaming, and Lonnie held him.

"What did you dream about?"

"I don't remember . . ."

"OK." She accepted his wall.

Bob was also in the army reserves. A few months after Baby's birth, Bob received his marching papers to go to Iraq. Patriotic and brave, he wanted to do his part to fight terrorism and protect his country. But even his police work never prepared him for the horror, shock, and panic of war. Roadside bombs blew his own men to pieces. Children he tried to shield one moment were skewered by shrapnel the next. He cried at first, then grew numb, except for the stabs of terror in his belly. The stress was unbearable. There was a woman soldier named Angela who worked beside him, cleaning up the debris of war. One night, after a particularly grueling day, they took comfort in each other's arms and bodies. Soon afterward, Bob was shipped home.

After his return, Bob immediately went back to work as a police officer. Then, one Sunday while sitting in a sidewalk restaurant with his family, a waiter quietly came up behind him to take his order. Bob sprang up, twisted in midair, lunged at the waiter, and grabbed his neck before he even knew what he was doing. The police were called.

Bob knew then he was in serious trouble. He reached out. With help, he learned that he was suffering from post-traumatic stress disorder, a malady common to combat veterans, but also to policemen and abused women, too.

Bob began to open up with Lonnie. As she held him night after night, he exposed his rawest wounds, the bloody images of war that plagued him. Finally, the night came when he took the biggest risk of all. He told Lonnie about Angela. Lonnie was crushed. She couldn't stop crying. For several weeks, Bob slept on the couch. They barely spoke. But over time, the wall between them thinned and faded. One morning a month later, they cried together while holding their baby. That day Lonnie called a therapist.

In counseling, they worked hard on listening, talking to one another, and soothing one another's hurts. Lonnie confessed stories she'd only told her sister, not Bob. Bob spilled out rage and fear from his years on the streets as a cop. They grew closer and deepened their friendship. And as they did, they rekindled their romance and passion.

Secrets held by both Lonnie and Bob had nearly destroyed them. Opening up and revealing the secrets saved them.

When we have a baby, our entire world changes. It is imperative that we bring our partner into this new world of ours. Share the shape-shifting. Trust that our partner's love will override the roller coaster of emotions we may convey. Talk.

10. Prioritize Gourmet Sex and Make Time for It

There's an old adage that a man needs sex to open up to love, but a woman needs love to open up to sex. In our study, most couples agreed. Our men said that something closed up inside them when they didn't feel sexually desired by their women. But our women complained that when their men didn't romance them, sex became just a chore. For both to be satisfied, they needed gourmet sex—the kind that is divinely delicious and takes time.

Romance and passion spring up from friendship. If we neglect romance and resort only to quickies, our sex becomes stale and stagnant. But when we confide in each other and know that we're loved, sex is the sweetest of all. Taking time for romance may seem like we're robbing our baby of time. But the fact is that

The greatest gift we can give our baby
is our love for each other

So the weekly dates, drives, picnics, or romantic dinners out alone not only nourish us, they benefit our babies as well. When our kids feel our love, they're happier. They're also learning, even as infants, what adult relationships look like, which they'll emulate later. Also, when we nurture our romance, *we're* happier. And happier grown-ups make better parents, whether playing individually or together with Baby. Unlike couples who neglect romance, we won't need to compete for Baby's attention, nor withdraw from Baby when we don't get it. Since babies love cooperative play with both parents, our babies will benefit the most if our relationship is sweet enough to spawn cooperative play—and it's romance that sugars the mix. Naturally, when we finally do sit down in that dark and intimate restaurant, all we'll talk about is Baby. That's fine! At least we'll be savoring the richness of new parenthood by ourselves, with candles lighting our smiles. And our passion.

In the next exercise, you'll have a chance to focus on ways to improve your sex life. Remember to say what you *do* need, not what you *don't* need. That way you'll deepen your trust and connection with one another. And you know where that can lead . . .

EXERCISE

HAVE THE CONVERSATIONS YOU NEED TO HAVE

INSTRUCTIONS. Both of you separately look over the following ten items. Pick one issue to discuss with your partner. Place a check mark in the box next to the area you select. Share with your partner the issue you've checked, and decide between you which one you'll discuss. Then talk about what changes you'dspecifically like to make in this area of your sexual relationship. Be gentle.

- Accept that things have changed since the baby arrived.

- Ask one another for sex.

- Talk about what feels good sexually, and how to make it better.

- Continue nonsexual affection, especially touch.

- Realize that in most cases, he's a microwave and she's a Dutch oven.

- Accept that quickies are as important as gourmet sex.

- Accept masturbation to orgasm, and continue to have oral sex (if you used to like it).

- Share your sexual fantasies.

- Discuss your innermost feelings and don't avoid conflict.

- Prioritize gourmet sex and make time for it.

14

ADD WARM FATHERING

DO WE REALLY NEED DADS?

In this day and age, babies can be born to women alone using sperm banks. And around the world, plenty of children need adopting. So do we really need fathers? If we look in the mirror of our culture today, the answer would be . . . no.

In most TV dramas, fathers are seen as bumbling and useless, or cold, strict, and punitive. Or just plain evil when they're authoritarian, dangerous, and violent. In sitcoms, they're immature fools and the brunt of jokes. Maybe that's better than commercials, where they're simply invisible. If the commercial is about parenting, females are 50 percent more likely to play the identified parent, 50 percent more likely to play a child's nurturer, and 600 percent more likely to play a child's parental teacher.

When it comes to the written word, more than half of all children's books name Mom as the only parent. And if Dad is mentioned, he is depicted as uncaring, unloving, absent, or irrelevant. In 64 percent of the books for very young children, dads get to be economic providers—only. And in books for kids in grades four to six, dads may be there, all right, but only as looming, scary authority figures.

ARE HUSBANDS NECESSARY?

Popular sociology hasn't helped men much. The term "the second shift" became a slogan from the mid-1960s on. It was used to describe working women who had two jobs, the second one at home. It also implied that when both men and women worked and returned home, husbands were slugs who sat on the couch channel surfing, while their wives cooked, cleaned, and cared for the kids.

The data that spawned the term "the second shift" in 1965 was actually collected in 1945. Although it totaled up men's and women's working hours on the job and at home, only weekday hours were counted, not hours on weekends. If weekend hours had been averaged in, employed fathers would have been seen to spend an average of ninety-one minutes a day in housework and child care. And that's without hours spent caring for kids through play. Furthermore, typically male-oriented activities were never mentioned, like mowing the lawn, maintaining the cars, and cleaning out gutters.

We know that men have a long way to go. However, largely due to the women's liberation movement, men's involvement at home has increased steadily since 1965. For example, studies find that men's time with kids averages almost 2 hours a day on weekdays and 6.5 hours a day on weekends—in all, 83 percent of the mother's time.

New dads also work more. Sociologist Steve Nock has shown that marriage propels men into achieving more at work. Also, men convert their fears about fathering into working harder. For example, the Family and Workforce Institute determined in 1997 that 96.8 percent of fathers work full-time compared with 73.2 percent of working mothers. Furthermore, "full-time" means an extra eight hours a week of paid work for fathers compared with mothers. In sum, we're not seeing any couch potatoes here. Everybody is working hard, on the job and at home.

Of course, household standards differ a lot between men and women. It's a revelation to most guys that the curtains ought to match the upholstery, or that curtains are a good idea at all. In a recent Broadway play, *Defending the Caveman,* the actor says that being married was his first time living with a woman. One day he came home and found his wife cleaning the bathroom. He said, "Are we moving?" As a single man, he had only wiped down a bathtub to get his security deposit back.

We've taped best friends playing together, starting with three-year-old children, up into the college years. Even little preschool boys and girls live in different worlds. In their fantasy play, little girls adore playing bride, house, and princess. They pretend to be mommies with doll babies in their arms. And they dress up in princess and bride regalia. But have you ever seen two little boys dressing up in their Sunday best and pretending to be bridegroom and best man?

No, little boys play hunter or hero. Listen to this conversation we taped between two little five-year-old boys playing at the kitchen sink.

A little blond towhead said, "Do you know how many things can kill you?"

"No, how many?" said his friend.

"About two jillion and five hundred, but the worst is the shark."

"He'd never get me, I'd swim away."

"Sharks can swim faster than you can. He eats you up in one bite."

"I'd run on land."

"Sharks can run on land faster than you can."

"I'd go behind a door."

"They can bite down a door."

"Not if it was metal."

"They can bite through metal."

"What should we do?"

"Let's go hunt him down before he gets us."

"Yeah."

There was a study that put preschool girls in a room with only metal toys and toy weapons, and preschool boys in a room with only baby dolls and stuffed animals. What would each gender do? The girls cradled the metal trucks in their arms like babies. The boys fired away at each other with baby-doll machine guns.

But later, when men set up house with their women, the wild beast gets tamed. How many men know how to help their brides-to-be select a pattern for china? The prospective groom learns to say, "Yeah, that one is lovely." "Lovely": a new word in the groom's vocabulary. And most moms easily figure out what is needed in Baby's nursery, while for guys this knowledge is hard to come by.

So if we're smart men, we'll accept influence from our women regarding home and baby care, and respect their standards.

And if we women want cooperative husbands, we'll back off our standards a bit and give our men some autonomy.

Want to see what your thoughts are about men as partners and dads? Take this self-test to find out.

SELF-TEST ON WHAT I BELIEVE ABOUT MEN

Circle either TRUE or FALSE box, depending on what you believe to be generally true.

1. Most men cannot be trusted to be faithful.	TRUE	FALSE
2. Women have to do most of the housework after Baby arrives.	TRUE	FALSE
3. Men rarely mature, and most of them remain boys.	TRUE	FALSE
4. You can't expect a man to be consistently involved with the baby.	TRUE	FALSE
5. Most men at the end of a day's work are couch potatoes.	TRUE	FALSE
6. A new father can't understand a baby's crying.	TRUE	FALSE
7. Most new fathers don't know what to do with a baby.	TRUE	FALSE
8. Most men aren't interested in the baby.	TRUE	FALSE

9. Men will always shirk the housework if they can.	TRUE	FALSE
10. Fathers aren't really necessary.	TRUE	FALSE
11. A woman needs a man like a fish needs a bicycle.	TRUE	FALSE
12. A father's play with Baby isn't very important.	TRUE	FALSE
13. Fathers can't be relied on to keep the baby totally safe.	TRUE	FALSE
14. A father is likely to forget the things kids need.	TRUE	FALSE
15. It is best to do things yourself and not rely on your baby's dad.	TRUE	FALSE

If you answered "True" four or more times, your attitude may be a problem for your relationship. Read on.

Now, try reflecting on your experience with your own dad. Perhaps it affects how you view your partner and his role as a dad today.

SELF-TEST ON MY DAD

Check either TRUE or FALSE, depending on your own relationship with your father.

1. My dad was not there for me.	TRUE	FALSE
2. My dad was cold; he wasn't warm.	TRUE	FALSE
3. My dad could be scary.	TRUE	FALSE
4. My dad hit me.	TRUE	FALSE
5. My dad had a real temper that scared me.	TRUE	FALSE
6. My dad said some mean things to me when I was little.	TRUE	FALSE
7. I really never understood my dad.	TRUE	FALSE
8. My dad was not affectionate.	TRUE	FALSE
9. My dad did not tell me he loved me.	TRUE	FALSE
10. My dad did not praise me.	TRUE	FALSE
11. My dad did not kiss or hug me.	TRUE	FALSE
12. My dad did not make me feel safe.	TRUE	FALSE

13. There was no pleasing my dad.	TRUE	FALSE
14. My dad never showed me he was proud of me.	TRUE	FALSE
15. My dad did not attend my special events (games, performances).	TRUE	FALSE
16. Sometimes I was scared of my dad.	TRUE	FALSE
17. My dad did not treat my mom very well.	TRUE	FALSE
18. My dad was violent toward me.	TRUE	FALSE
19. My dad had a problem with alcohol or drugs.	TRUE	FALSE
20. My dad sometimes favored other siblings of mine over me.	TRUE	FALSE
21. My dad was unfair.	TRUE	FALSE
22. My dad neglected me.	TRUE	FALSE
23. I avoided my dad whenever I could.	TRUE	FALSE
24. To this day, I am upset about how my dad treated me.	TRUE	FALSE
25. I never really knew my dad.	TRUE	FALSE
26. My dad never really knew or understood me.	TRUE	FALSE

Add up the number of items you checked "True." If your total is greater than 5, it may be hard for you to know what a good father is like. Read on to find out.

DO WE NEED FATHERS?

The answer is yes. Fathers provide children with a bounty of gifts. Research reveals that fathers offer infants more freedom to explore while moms promote precautions. Michael Yogman and T. Berry Brazelton, both pediatricians, found that Father's play is more physical and tactile, while Mom's play is more visual and verbal. Father's play has fits and starts, while Mom's play is more steady and even. And psychologists Hildy Ross and Heather Taylor discovered that because babies love dads' jazzy approach, two-thirds of two-and-a-half-year-olds choose dads as play partners over moms. Plainly put, dads are just more fun.

In our study, we saw that moms persist in a particular game even if Baby isn't interested. For example, "Who is the tallest in the zoo?" says one mom to a seven-month-old baby as she shows him a picture of a giraffe. He crawls away. He doesn't care about the giraffe. She circles around him and shows him the picture again. And again he crawls away. Mom is relentless. She tries again. As Baby again retreats, we hear him sigh and say, "Ah, Mama . . ." But Mom was just being Baby's patient teacher.

Dads are different. They drop a game like a hot potato if Baby crawls away. So if Baby picks up a truck, Dad immediately says, "Vroom, vroom," to get into Baby's new game. Then Dad *becomes* a tow truck, hoisting Baby up onto his back, rolling on the floor, and tumbling and tickling Baby as Baby squeals with delight. While moms are guides, dads are playmates. And babies need both.

There's more. Dads can be sweet and gentle, too. Studies have shown that moms caress their sons more than dads, but dads caress their daughters more than moms. So we seem to need both moms and dads at the helm. It's a balance.

Does Dad's play style help Baby to develop? Again, the answer is *yes*. Dads' rough-and-tumble play generates babies' self-control abilities. In studies of young children, the high-energy, positive play of dads predicts how well kids are viewed and accepted by their peers. Our own data show that if dads are involved in their children's emotional world at age four (we call this "emotion coaching"), the kids are more socially competent at age eight. Scores of other studies have yielded similar results.

Here's one of our favorite examples. In the 1950s, a brilliant psychologist named Robert Sears did research on three hundred families when the kids were five years old. Twenty-six years later, three other psychologists reassessed the kids from these families who were now thirty-one-year-old adults. They asked, what factors in the children's world predicts their becoming empathic adults later? The best predictor of empathy turned out to be dads' involvement with their children at age five, whether the kids were sons or daughters. Ten years later, when they were forty-one, these kids were again studied. This time the question was, who has the best social relationships in midlife with spouses, kids, and community? Again, it was the kids who experienced more of their dads' warmth when they were little. From ages five to forty-one, Dad's involvement made the difference.

Research has also demonstrated that fathers' skill in playing infant games like peekaboo and ball toss predicts more intellectually advanced kids later. Children with actively involved fathers also have higher verbal ability and IQ scores and better academic performance in third grade. There seems to be a magic formula: Dads need to be emotionally accessible and responsive. Just being there isn't enough, for dads can be absent even when they're present. At the other end of the spectrum, a harsh, cold, authoritarian, and punitive dad can greatly damage his kids' emotional and intellectual development. So, a child will do best if his dad is involved, playful, caring, and, above all, *warm.*

Children aren't the only ones who gain from good dads. Wives are happier, too, and their parenting shines when their husbands are warm and responsive dads.

Mind you, it doesn't take a male to be a good dad. Either gender can do it. One study trained moms to play with babies like dads usually do, and trained dads to play with babies like moms usually do. Guess what? The babies preferred moms over dads as playmates. So women can learn to be good dads, too. It just doesn't come as naturally to women as to men.

Peggy Sanday is an anthropologist who studied parenting and partnering in 194 hunting-gathering cultures. She learned that hierarchical families flourish during dangerous times. When food is scarce and predators are plentiful, men dominate their women and their kids. They stay distant from their daughters and link up with their sons only after adolescent rites of passage.

But in safer climes where peace prevails, dads and moms enjoy egalitarian partnerships, and dads help nurture the babies. And the reverse, she found, is also true! When dads and moms equally share in child care, and symbols of the female are religiously honored, there is also less war. Not surprisingly, Sanday found that cultures like these are also less likely to die out.

What Sanday hinted at is profoundly important. In a safe environment, if men treat their women as equals, take a nurturing role with their babies, and honor both male and female in their sacred traditions, perhaps war can be eliminated altogether. It could look like this: A dad says, "What is this war about? . . . Oh, sorry, no, not a good enough reason. You're not taking my baby!"

Think about it. In the West, our environs are mostly safe. No predators roam the streets, except for the occasional human. And food is gathered in grocery stores; they let men in those stores, not just women.

Second, women are empowering themselves all over the world—psychologically, socially, economically, and politically—despite backlash reactions to stop them.

Third, in the United States, 91 percent of men are attending the births of their babies, and college men are taking classes on family in unprecedented numbers. Thirty years ago, only women would have attended our "Bringing Baby Home" workshops. Now men initiate attending it half the time.

Finally, the female is once again being honored religiously. Many Catholics directly pray to the Virgin Mary. And many Jews honor the matriarchs and the female spirit of God, called the Shechinah.

Perhaps our culture is truly at a crossroads. If we dedicate ourselves to involving our dads more in child care, peace may be within reach. But there are cultural forces working against father involvement that we must be more aware of.

FATHERS ARE OFTEN
EXCLUDED IN OUR CULTURE

No one is more surprised about the importance of fathers than fathers. When we speak to audiences of dads, they are rapt with astonishment at the facts. Are they really that important to both their sons' and daughters' development? Moms are equally surprised, like a woman at one of our talks. She said that when her husband came home and got down on the floor to play with the kids, she would get angry. She'd complain, "Hey! I have been doing so much all day, and here all you're doing is playing. Pitch in and help out!" But now she knew he *was* making a contribution—through play with the kids. In the future, maybe she'd just voice her appreciation, and ask for help with the chores later.

Circles of women are also inclined to swoop in around a new mom. With experience and expertise, they gently help with Baby and push Dad out. Most dads are only too happy to leave. Who needs poopy diapers? But dads don't realize that feeding, bathing, diapering, and dressing babies create lovely opportunities for connection, play, and fun. Once dads discover this magic, they never want to leave. Unfortunately, many dads depart too soon. They may get excluded by women, but they exclude themselves, too.

These days, however, there's a new movement afoot. Dads are seeking to include themselves, right from the beginning. In delivery rooms across America, 91 percent of fathers witness the births of their babies. A generation ago, that percentage was zero, since hospitals didn't permit fathers in the delivery room. Does it matter? You bet. Research has shown that dads' presence in the delivery room heightens couples' birth experience and reduces hostility between moms and dads later.

So what has changed? Has the medical community suddenly attained enlightenment about including dads? Or have dads only recently changed? Hardly. The past holds some keys to this evolution in fathering. Let's begin our story with the history of childbirth.

THE HISTORY OF CHILDBIRTH

For many centuries, dating back to ancient times, children were born at home, and extremely competent women known as midwives and doulas aided them. Midwives were experts in the physical and medical processes of pregnancy, birth, and healing. They were there for moms before, during, and after delivery, and they managed difficult births. Doulas provided emotional support. They held, comforted, and massaged moms. They also answered questions and spoke gently to offer moms reassurance. Note the absence of men in this circle.

Then, in the late Middle Ages, the Catholic Church aimed the spear of antipaganism at the bellies of women. Pagan religions revered women. Women could be visionaries, sages, healers, and midwives. But in 1484, the pope sanctified a book called *The Hammer of Witches* (*Malleus maleficarum*), published by two German Dominican monks, Heinrich Kramer and Jakob Sprenger. *The Hammer* was filled with hateful denunciations of women. It said that women fornicated with the Devil in open fields, where "black smoke rose from their thighs."

The Hammer also claimed that women turned into succubi at night and sucked up men's power, provoked their wet dreams, and drove them mad. It blamed female witches for everything from crop failures and cows going dry to any male despondency, or loss of vigor or sexual potency.

Under the authority of this document, monks robed as inquisitors rooted out women healers and midwives, tried them under torture, and burned them at the stake. The Church also invited men to turn in their own mates, and many men did—a gruesome way to rid themselves of unwanted wives.

Church inquisitors would arrive in a town accompanied by expert torturers, set up their "court," and begin hearing local complaints. Soon afterward, convicted women would be burned to death. When all was finished, the inquisitors would travel on to the next town. The Inquisition blanketed Europe, snuffing out women in almost every town.

It is now estimated by historians that fifty thousand women, mostly healers and midwives, were tortured and murdered as a result of *The Hammer.* Yet despite mass murder and the Church's deployment of male physicians, mothers continued to call on midwives to help with the delivery of their babies.

In the sixteenth century, the first group of male midwives appeared, formed by the Guild of Barbers and Surgeons. It was led by a very strange man named Peter Chamberlen. In 1588, Mr. Chamberlen invented the childbirth forceps, and he and then his family kept its design a secret for two hundred years. Male midwives employed the forceps to forcibly pull a baby out of its mother by its head. The tool was touted as a marvel for complicated births, and the Chamberlen family grew rich and famous through its invention. Meanwhile, female midwives still quietly carried on their delivery practices, without the forceps.

COMBATING INFECTION

Amazingly enough, during the late eighteenth century pregnancy began to be viewed as a disease. A doctor named Joseph De Lee summed it up: "It always strikes physicians as well as laymen as bizarre to call labor an abnormal function, and yet it is a decidedly pathological process."

Around the same time, upper-class English women started to worry about birth complications. Worst-case birth scenarios had been widely publicized, and they were terrified. Apparently, childbirth could usher them to "death's door."

Following their doctors' advice, these women fled to hospitals in droves to deliver their children. In hospitals, they could avoid birth complications, their doctors preached. In reality, however, birth complications were few. Midwives had been handling them in homes for generations.

Across Europe, lower-class urban women flocked to hospitals, too. But a striking phenomenon followed. Whatever the class, women delivering in hospitals also began dying in hospitals. They were contracting an infection called puerperal fever, which, at the time, was fatal.

Now into our story steps the brilliant Dr. Ignaz Semmelweis, a true scientist. In Vienna, where the good doctor worked, there were two hospitals where women delivered their babies. The so-called First Hospital was staffed by doctors who delivered babies either after seeing other live but sick patients or doing autopsies on dead patients. In contrast, the so-called Second Hospital was staffed entirely by midwives whose sole job was to deliver babies.

Dr. Semmelweis noticed that the deadly fever consumed mothers four times more often in the hospital staffed by doctors than in the hospital staffed by midwives. He unearthed a recommendation made by Joseph Lister twenty years earlier: Use antiseptics in the surgery room. Dr. Semmelweis had doctors at First Hospital wash their hands in chloride of lime solution before delivering a baby, which cleansed them of the germs from other festering patients. And the rate of puerperal fever plummeted.

Now the medical community bellowed its objections. A doctor is a gentleman, and of course gentlemen have clean hands, they said. Semmelweis was out to undermine the confidence patients have in their doctors. Furthermore, he sought to drown the sterling reputation of his fellows. As a result of these smears, instead of garnering applause and gratitude, Semmelweis was drummed out of medicine. He died in poverty.

In the United States, however, a famous physician, Dr. Oliver Wendell Holmes, picked up the gauntlet and carried on Semmelweis's cause. Holmes also encountered great opposition from fellow doctors. Unlike Semmelweis, though, he triumphed over their objections, and antiseptic hospital deliveries became the standard.

By 1860, more pregnant upper-class women were demanding the services of doctors. But we're talking about Victorian times here. At first, male doctors would grope under the large petticoats of their modest female patients to avoid looking at their genitals. This practice didn't survive long, thankfully.

The next giant step forward in medical childbirth involved anesthesia. Dr. James Young Simpson introduced chloroform into the surgery room. Simpson was a character with a twisted sense of humor. He used chloroform to put himself out at dinner parties. He also put out some of his hapless dinner guests, much to the delight of those remaining vertical. And, of course, he continually terrorized his poor sister, whom he chased around the house with a bottle of chloroform. Despite Simpson's "charm," other doctors saw the benefits of chloroform, too, and began using it regularly during childbirth to ease the pains of labor.

Yet even the practice of easing labor pains was greeted with great controversy. In England's premier medical journal, the *Lancet*, doctors wrote that this unnatural procedure could hurt both the baby and the mother. Clergymen raised their voices against it, too. They reminded people that in the Bible, painful births were women's punishment for the sin of Eve, who had eaten an apple from the Tree of Knowledge. How blasphemous for women to think that they shouldn't have to bear God's decreed punishment. Queen Victoria, however, disagreed. During the birth of her eighth child, she took "that blessed chloroform." Thereafter, opposition to its use evaporated.

Other medical innovations followed. For example, in 1882, Dr. Max Sänger pioneered successful Cesarean sections in Germany.

It took time for women to embrace the new. Most moms still delivered their babies at home with the assistance of midwives. By 1900, only 5 percent of all births took place in hospitals. But by 1939, the figures rose to 75 percent for women in cities and 50 percent for women overall. And by 1970, nearly 100 percent of women journeyed to hospitals to deliver their children.

Remember, though, that fathers who were excluded from child-birth by midwives were also shut out by doctors. So how did they wind up in the delivery room?

THE HISTORY OF DADS IN THE DELIVERY ROOM

These days in the United States, a massive 91 percent of fathers attend the birth of their babies. Fifty years ago, that figure was zero percent. It all started in 1957 with a letter published in the *Ladies' Home Journal*. A nurse took pen to paper to expose what she called the cruel and sadistic treatment of women during childbirth.

In the months that followed, hundreds of letters poured in. The editor described them as "so shocking they deserve national attention." One woman wrote that she was rushed into the labor room where her arms and legs were strapped down with leather cuffs. Then she was left alone for eight hours until the actual delivery. As she screamed in pain, nurses repeatedly ordered her to be quiet. This experience, it turned out, was typical.

In 1962, the *New York Times* quoted a doctor, J. H. Patterson, who said that when a man's wife is delivering, the proper place for him to be is in a bar. And the bartender's role is to take the phone call that tells the gentleman whether his wife has delivered a boy or a girl. Then the father can pay for a round of drinks and pass out cigars to the other men at the bar.

The same article reported that New York City hospitals forbade fathers' presence during delivery; many doctors claimed that they could not predict men's behavior during childbirth. Fathers could be potentially dangerous. At best, they were distracting. And birthing was now an assembly-line process, the *Times* said. The (usually male) doctor often attended the delivery of several babies at once. The births were controlled by administering oxytocin, a drug to expedite labor. In short, disregard and cruelty flourished in the delivery room; compassion and caring were nowhere in sight.

However, change was brewing. As early as 1933, Dr. Grantly Dick-Read wrote in his book *Childbirth Without Fear* that the presence of fathers during childbirth could be positive. In the 1950s, Dr. Fernand Lamaze agreed. In 1958 in Seattle, Clifford and Audrey Stone sued Group Health Cooperative so that Clifford could be with his wife during childbirth. In Denver, Dr. Robert Bradley permitted fathers in the delivery room to coach and calm down their "hysterical" wives. He reasoned, "Let's face a fact: they [pregnant women] are nuttier than a fruitcake."

Moms and dads were the real change agents. In 1955 in Seattle, parents formed an organization called the Seattle Association for Childbirth Education (SACE). Joan Patten, the wife of a Boeing Aircraft engineer, was its first president. On April 25, 1955, SACE produced a twenty-minute color and sound film called *Childbirth as a Family Experience.* The *Seattle Times* said that the film was created by "a group convinced that father should have more to do with childbirth than paying the bills."

A couple's actual labor and delivery were shown on the film. SACE took the film to the Maternity Center Association in New York, where it was shown to five hundred parent-delegates from the United States and Canada. Afterward, at the Seattle YWCA, SACE began to offer birth preparation classes that included dads. Of course, everywhere outside of Seattle, SACE was skewered for its precocity.

Then on September 22, 1960, in Arcata, California, a twenty-three-year-old student at Humboldt State University chained himself to his nineteen-year-old laboring wife, Carole. The *San Francisco Chronicle* reported that earlier, young John Quinn told the attending physician, Dr. Henry Frank, that he wanted to be with his wife. Allegedly, Dr. Frank replied, "Impossible." Mr. Quinn smiled gently and proceeded to handcuff himself to Carole. He said, "This is my wife. I love her. I want to be there."

The hospital called the cops. As officer Don Mann stood there scratching his head and trying to decide what to do, a healthy eight-pound baby boy was born. Afterward, Mr. Quinn unlocked the padlocks and departed peacefully. No one filed any charges. "We just told him that from now on, he'd simply have to observe our rules," the hospital administrator said.

Hospitals heard about Mr. Quinn's "crime." They responded by tightening up their policies. But the debate was on, heard in medical communities across the country. In the *New York Times*, Hazel Corbin, who directed the New York City Maternity Center, reported increasing requests from couples for names of hospitals that permitted dads in delivery rooms.

Virginia Mason Medical Center in Seattle responded to those families. By the late 1960s, a whopping 80 percent of fathers attended the births of their babies after hearing lectures and movies to prepare them beforehand.

Changes in childbirth skyrocketed. Delivery rooms were softly lit. Music was played. Birth preparation classes were attended by fathers, and obstetricians expected dads to be present during delivery. Progress was long in coming, but it had finally arrived for dads.

THE SECRET TO DAD'S INVOLVEMENT WITH THE BABY

About ten years ago, it was a bit depressing to ask what could be done to get fathers more involved with their babies. For example, there was one study that showed that if you taught dads in hospitals how to feed their newborns, the dads would become a little more involved with Baby, but only with sons, not with daughters. So what was the answer?

Myron Levine and Robert Block, two obstetricians, supervised dads in delivering their own babies (provided there were no birth complications, of course). They discovered that these dads became twice as involved with their three-month-old babies as dads who'd not had this experience. But facilitating involvement could also be as subtle as shifting hours. In a London study, when pediatricians had early evening office hours available, dads were twice as likely to bring their kids in for medical visits.

Then the research took a sharp left turn. A number of studies uncovered a relationship between Dad's involvement with Baby and the amount of conflict he had with Baby's mom. Over and over again, in every class, ethnic, and racial group in the United States, the findings were echoed. If conflict was ferocious with Mom and relationship satisfaction between parents was low, Dad withdrew from both Mom *and* Baby. If there was little conflict with Mom, Dad stayed more involved with both.

This research was tremendously helpful. It told us that moms and dads relating well to one another could help dads stay involved with their babies. But could we take it a step further? Could we flip the equation? Could we actually increase Dad's involvement with Baby *by* improving his relationship with Mom? And could we make it happen on a wide scale, across multiple layers of society? What if we changed hospitals so that they supported couples not only on the day of delivery, but on every day, after that? We decided to try.

OUR FINDINGS

When we began this work, we knew it was all a big gamble. We developed the "Bringing Baby Home" workshop, then kept our fingers crossed and our hearts hopeful.

Sure enough—it's several years now—we've found that the combination of reducing conflict with Mom, making inevitable conflicts constructive, maintaining intimacy between Mom and Dad, and providing tools to help Dad with Baby is the grand slam we've been looking for. Here's the score this combo produces.

- *Dad's increased involvement with Mom*
- *Dad's increased involvement with Baby*

- *Dad's greater positive feelings towards his three-month-old son or daughter*
- *Baby's greater interest in both Mom and Dad during play*
- *Longer-lasting playtimes with Baby*
- *Less hostility between Mom and Dad*
- *Greater relationship satisfaction between Mom and Dad*
- *Fewer symptoms of postpartum depression in Mom*
- *Greater satisfaction for both Mom and Dad in parenting*
- *Baby's better emotional development*
- *Baby's better intellectual development*

IMPLICATIONS FOR HERE AND NOW

Like new cedars springing up, men are growing into wonderful fathers—rapidly. Men of every color, class, and ethnicity are dedicating themselves to being better partners and fathers than their fathers were. We've seen it in middle-class white men in the great poet Robert Bly's men's movement. We've seen it in black men in the Million Man March on Washington. We've seen it in the football stadiums where thousands of politically conservative white men in the Promise Keepers movement sing songs about being better husbands and fathers. There is a new father emerging in America.

We see it now as we go around the country training devoted leaders to facilitate relationship and family workshops for impoverished married and unmarried couples who have just had a baby. Men of so many of our diverse cultures are all declaring that they will be good fathers. They'll be consistently in their children's lives, like the fathers they never had. And they'll honor the mothers of their babies so their children can see a successful relationship between parents.

One father in Florida tells us that he is twenty-six years old; he's been in prison for eight of those years. In prison, he was over a thousand miles away from his daughters. Now that he's out, he vows he'll never be apart from them again. After his release, he asked the mother of his eleven-year-old to let him back into his daughter's life. The mom hated him, so it wasn't easy. Eventually, she agreed to let him see her. It was easier with the mom of the seven-year-old. Now he regularly sees her, too. As he talks, he cradles his new baby, and his new woman wraps her arms around him. He says he is working three jobs now. He isn't about to leave.

Another father in Baltimore tells us that every now and then, he glances out his living-room window at the street corner where he once made $20,000 a week dealing drugs. Some months now, he can't pay the rent. But he is holding down two jobs, he's not going to jail, and he never walks down the street carrying a gun. He is staying with his wife, who is his "queen." Together they are building a family that encircles his mother, his baby, his other son, and their church—the church he once cursed.

It is the same story, told and retold, a vast change in just one generation. Men are stepping up to the plate. They are meeting the new challenge started by the women's movement forty-five years ago—that they become better partners and friends, and stay involved with their babies. They are succeeding.

A TOOL FOR DAD

This next exercise is for dads who want to be more involved with their kids. Of course, involvement takes planning. And care. Here's how you can add the warm fathering that will nourish both you and your family.

ADD WARM FATHERING

INSTRUCTIONS. Dad, look over the *very long* list below. There are 167 items on this list. We purposely made the list long so that you can have lots of choices in how to be more involved with your kids and helpful to your partner.

Pick six ways in which you'd like to be more involved. Try to make two of these chores, and four of them parenting activities. Then talk over your choices with your partner and make a plan for increasing your involvement. Be sure to accept influence from one another during your discussion.

Mom, when Dad does the items he's chosen, try not to have superhigh standards. Give appreciation for what is done, because the more your partner feels appreciated, the better he'll feel about what he's doing.

And both of you, remember: Turning toward leads to more turning toward.

Here's what I'd like to do as a dad. (Dad, pick six things: two chores, and four kid items. Talk these over with Mom. Make a plan.)

- Tell a kid how much you love him or her.
- Hug or kiss a kid.
- Plan a special outing with one kid.
- Find something to compliment or praise about what a kid did.
- Bring a kid a special gift.
- Do the breakfast dishes.
- Do the dinner dishes.
- Set the table.
- Clean the counters.
- Mop the kitchen floor.
- Dust the house (which rooms?).
- Vacuum the house.
- Clean the floors.
- Clean the bathroom.

- Clean out the garage.
- Keep the car in good repair.
- Clean out the basement.
- Cook dinner.
- Make the kids' lunches.
- Make breakfast.
- Put gas and oil in the car.
- Cook a holiday meal.
- Take out the garbage.
- Maintain the outside of our home.
- Sweep the outside.
- Change the oil in the car.
- Do (or get done) the car tune-up.
- Wash the car.
- Do a special home project.
- Change the baby's diaper.
- Feed the baby.
- Get up with the baby at night.
- Calm a distressed child or baby.
- Get the baby dressed.
- Bathe the baby.
- Play with the baby.
- Take a child to a doctor's appointment.
- Take the children to school.
- Pick the kids up from school.
- Make sure the kids have everything they need when they leave for the day.
- Drive a kid to a place he or she needs to go.
- Get the baby or kids to sleep at night.

- Make the beds.
- Praise a kid for a job well done.
- Do the laundry.
- Plan a visit to relatives.
- Read to kids at night.
- Put away the laundry.
- Do the grocery shopping.
- Pick up medicines we need.
- Clean up the yard.
- Do the weeding.
- Take care of the pet's health.
- Take the dog for a walk.
- Make sure the doors and windows are locked at night.
- Turn off all the lights when not needed.
- Do repair work around the house.
- Help a kid with homework.
- Clean out the refrigerator or freezer.
- Water the plants.
- Tidy up the common living areas.
- Put away the kid toys.
- Calm the baby when he or she is crying.
- Turn off the TV and talk to Mom.
- Turn off the TV and talk to a kid.
- Get people presents.
- Keep in touch with kin.
- Prepare for a holiday.
- Run errands to the cleaners.
- Wash the windows.
- Plan the week's food menu.

- Go grocery shopping.
- Clean up after dinner.
- Clean the kitchen.
- Put out clean towels.
- Keep counters clean.
- Tidy up generally.
- Deal with car mechanics.
- Sort incoming mail.
- Pay the bills.
- Balance the checkbook.
- Write letters.
- Take phone messages.
- Return phone calls or e-mail.
- Save some money.
- Take out garbage and trash.
- Recycle.
- Iron clothes.
- Mend clothes.
- Put the clean clothes away.
- Sweep kitchen and eating area.
- Vacuum.
- Wash and wax floors.
- Put dirty laundry away.
- Change lightbulbs.
- Repair appliances.
- Make the beds.
- Defrost and clean refrigerator.
- Shop for kid clothing.
- Plan travel or outing.

- Take charge of one home repair.
- Take charge of a remodel.
- Do some home maintenance.
- Buy some furniture we need.
- Redecorate part of our home.
- Buy an item for the home.
- Buy a new appliance for the home.
- Sew and mend something that needs it (or get it done by laundry).
- Straighten kitchen cabinets.
- Do yard and garden work.
- Do lawn, tree, or shrubbery maintenance.
- Do an errand to the bank.
- Do some houseplant care.
- Straighten and rearrange a closet.
- Get house ready for guests.
- Do party preparations.
- Plan a vacation.
- Plan a getaway for just Mom and Dad.
- Plan a romantic date.
- Plan a quiet evening at home.
- Plan a weekend event (like a drive or a picnic).
- Plan a special meal (could be takeout).
- Coach a kid sport.
- Start a general conversation with Mom.
- Have a conversation with a kid.
- Plan a romantic evening.
- Initiate lovemaking.
- Initiate talking about how to improve our lovemaking.
- Plan a dinner out.

- Plan a family outing, a drive, or a picnic.
- Do some financial planning.
- Plan a major purchase (car, etc.).
- Work on managing an investment.
- Talk about relationship with Mom.
- Plan a get-together with friends.
- Keep in touch with friends.
- Do the taxes.
- Handle a legal matter (e.g., wills).
- Plan a part of our family's medicine/health.
- Get the drugs we need or do other health errands (drugstore pickups).
- Plan exercise and fitness for everyone.
- Plan a recreational outing.
- Spend time with Baby.
- Plan a family outing with the baby.
- Handle a visit to the pediatrician.
- Handle a visit to the dentist or orthodontist.
- Help with child homework.
- Handle a child bath.
- Handle the child discipline.
- Do bedtime with the baby.
- Deal with a sick child.
- Handle a child crisis.
- Deal with a child's negative emotions.
- Set limits with a kid.
- Attend a kid special event (game, performance).
- Attend a teacher conference.
- Deal with the school.
- Attend a special kid or parent event at school.

Add Warm Fathering

- Plan a kid birthday or other party.
- Arrange a kid lesson (like music).
- Arrange a kid playdate.
- Shop for baby or kid stuff.
- Buy children gifts.
- Take children to school.
- Pick up children from school.
- Arrange child care after school.
- Do child meals and lunches.

15

BAKE THE BREAD OF LEGACY

We human beings are not simple creatures. Ironically, our mating and bearing children uproots our lives in a way that's difficult to imagine. It's not enough to simply cohabit, manage conflict, and be friends. There's a restlessness inside us that compels us to seek meaning, to build something beyond ourselves and our simple existence.

In our study, the couples that sailed through the turbulent rapids of Baby's arrival looked for mooring, for goals and values that anchored them. In adapting to family life with its constant twists and turns, they shifted their balance, grabbed hold of new oars, mapped out their destination, and navigated toward their new goals together. They filled their lives with purpose and meaning.

It didn't start out that way. When childless, each partner had his or her own values and traditions that were embedded in personal history. But having children changed all that. Who would pilot the child's ship? Whose values would serve as the North Star? How would the couple map out the family's future course? What personal traditions would be shed, and which ones would be embraced? How would they create a family legacy that would ferry their child forward into a good life? The couples who did best struggled with questions like these. It's not that they arrived at a set of enlightened answers. Rather, they grounded themselves by asking the questions.

In other words, the routines of daily life weren't enough. They wanted more. They'd worked hard to cool down their conflicts, create nourishing friendships, and heat up their sex lives. They'd added warm fathering to the mix. They had all the right ingredients. But what to create? Not just any family. They wanted one with substance, one that was tasty but nourished their souls and the souls of their children, too. Intentionally, they thought about the shape of their family life, the weight of it, and who else it might feed besides themselves. They thought of its beauty. They wanted it to contain what was most central to each of them. So they took strands from their own individual cultures and wove them together into a beautiful braided bread. Not one full of holes, but one dense and thick with purpose and meaning. The couples who did best were marvelous bakers.

THE FIRST STRAND: SHIFTING FROM ME TO WE

In our first "Bringing Baby Home" study, done thirteen years ago, we followed 130 newlywed couples in Seattle as some became pregnant and had babies. In the sixth month of pregnancy, we inquired about what the pregnancy had been like for them, how they felt about Baby's imminent arrival, and so on.

The most dramatic result was this: Couples who did well after the baby arrived became a team early on, during the pregnancy. Each one didn't just think about "ME." They thought of themselves as "WE." They made sacrifices for the "team" that they would never have made before becoming pregnant. Men played a central role, and the "ME-to-WE" men were easy to spot. They praised their women, they loved how their pregnant women looked, and they supported their women throughout the pregnancy. They sympathized if their women had stomach troubles, they brought them extra pillows if they were uncomfortable, and they helped more with housework if their women needed rest. With both partners shifting from ME to WE, couples sailed easily through the transition into parenthood.

Other couples had a rougher time of it. The men complained about the pregnancy experience. They felt put upon, and they left their women feeling unattractive and lonely. Like in the Beatles' song "I Me Mine," they never moved from ME to WE, and their family life suffered as a consequence.

For example, Leon and Tammy were interviewed during their sixth month of pregnancy. Leon announced a plan to go skiing. The incredulous interviewer asked, "You guys are going skiing?"

"No," said Tammy. "Just Leon's going."

"Yeah," Leon added. "I see no reason to put a stop to my sports interests just because she's pregnant."

When asked about the experience of pregnancy, Tammy said that it had been very hard. Nervously, she joked that she looked fat.

"Uh-huh," chortled Leon. "She looks like a whale. Both of us prided ourselves on being in shape before this. And now she's truly a fat person."

Tammy flushed and looked down. Leon was still in the ME phase. Not surprisingly, this family didn't do well later on.

Another couple, Greg and Sara, also commented on physical change during pregnancy. Greg said, "Physical changes . . . medically I understand what's going on and I realize we're both pretty health conscious and all that, but we always have looked down on fat people, and suddenly my wife—"

Sara interrupted him. "Not looked down!"

"Well, OK, not 'looked down.'"

Sara explained that they had always been thin. "It's something we've never had to worry about, either one of us."

Attempting a repair, Greg added, "And, you know, I realize this extra weight is not total fat, but it's just like—"

"Buddha-esque is what you called me the other day," Sarah interrupted. She didn't laugh. This also didn't bode well.

During pregnancy, too little WE-ness and too much criticism of the women's appearance pollutes couples' conflicts. For instance, when Greg and Sara were asked to discuss a problem in the lab, they had a horrible fight. They hammered each other for the stresses they were undergoing. In our lab six months later, their relationship satisfaction scores had traveled south. Moreover, their three-month-old baby cried a lot and laughed little. When they were asked to play with him, their play was out of sync and they competed for his attention. During the play session, the baby became overstimulated, upset, and couldn't continue. Their family future didn't look bright.

In contrast, there were couples like Phil and Sheanna. Phil talked about how beautiful Sheanna looked, remarking, "She just glows." Men like Phil frequently complimented their women. Some even said they felt romantic about being pregnant. They talked to the baby inside Mom's tummy and delighted in feeling the baby move. It is stressful being pregnant, they commented, but they coped with it together. They sometimes said, "We're pregnant." That's the shift from ME to WE.

When we analyzed our findings from the lab, the transition to becoming a team, or a WE, was an index of how well couples coped with being pregnant. This index predicted the couple's satisfaction with their relationship later. It also amazingly predicted what kind of baby couples would have—one who would cry and be distressed, or one who would smile and laugh. It really behooved couples to become a WE.

During the couples' pregnancy-month-six visit to our lab, we looked at two other facets of our couples. First, we showed them a video of a happy baby and a video of a crying baby in random order. As they watched these videos, we measured their physiological response—how fast their hearts beat and how fast their blood flowed. Six months later, when their babies were three months old, we asked the parents to tell us how much their baby smiled, laughed, or was distressed and cried. Our graduate student Eun Young Nahm analyzed this data.

We knew from a study by psychologists Ann Frodi and Michael Lamb that moms' heart rates could vary while watching tapes like these. Frodi and Lamb found that heart rates of child-abusing moms escalated while watching either tapes of crying babies *or* tapes of happy, cooing babies. However, the heart rates of non-child-abusing moms increased *only* with the tape of crying babies but *decreased* when viewing a tape of happy babies. In short, unlike nonabusing moms, child-abusing moms were negatively aroused by any baby, no matter what its emotional state.

In our study, we had no child-abusing moms or dads. But our results paralleled these, plus taking us one step further. During the sixth month of pregnancy, the women who had slower heart rates and blood velocities while viewing the happy-baby film gave birth to babies who were later less distressed and cranky. Also, the men who had slower heart rates and blood velocities while watching either baby film had three-month-old babies who often smiled and laughed. The physiology of parents during pregnancy later predicted the temperament of their babies. We scratched our heads. How did this work?

The answer appeared when we looked at how the pregnant couples dealt with conflict. During the sixth month of pregnancy, we had videotaped the same couples trying to resolve an ongoing disagreement. Another graduate student, Alyson Shapiro, discovered that the more unhappy the couples were in their sixth month of pregnancy and the more hostile their conflict discussion, the more their three-month-old babies would cry and the less they would laugh during face-to-face play. These babies were less able to physiologically calm down and soothe themselves, too. In contrast, the parents who eased through their earlier conflict discussions had three-month-old babies who smiled more, laughed more, and cried less during play. These babies were neurologically and emotionally better equipped to calm down, focus attention, and self-soothe.

Here's some relevant information: A baby's ability to self-soothe and to focus attention is controlled by the development of an important nerve in the body, the vagus nerve, which is the tenth cranial nerve. The better the baby's "vagal tone," the better this ability.

When Alyson analyzed her data, she found that half the variation in the baby's vagal tone could be accounted for by the quality of the parents' conflict discussion while the baby was still in Mom's womb. That's a very powerful prediction! In other words, the quality of a couple's marital relationship and how they handle conflicts while pregnant will determine, in part, what kind of baby they'll have. If they handle conflicts well and relate to each other well, they're more likely to have a happy baby who can self-soothe and focus attention.

The big news for us is that the quality of our marital relationship while pregnant is literally tailoring our baby's temperament.

Back in the lab, we made another groundbreaking discovery when we analyzed the results of our "Bringing Baby Home" workshop. We found that if we could alter partners' ME attitude to a WE attitude and hone their conflict skills, we could increase their chances of having a baby with a good temperament. It looked like the "Bringing Baby Home" workshop may have altered the conditions in Mom's uterus, for the betterment of both parents and baby.

Shifting from being a ME to a WE can make a difference. Would you like to try it? Then look at this next exercise.

EXERCISE

FROM ME TO WE

INSTRUCTIONS. To begin to build WE-ness, identify the one area you would both like to work on together.

First, fill out the following questionnaire individually. Look over each item. Fill in a number between 1 and 5 to indicate how much you would like to build toward WE-ness in that area (1=we are fine in this area and there is absolutely no need to build more WE-ness; 2=perhaps there's a slight need to build more WE-ness; 3=there's a moderate need to build more WE-ness; 4=indicates a strong need to build more WE-ness; 5=it is very important to build more WE-ness). Then add up your circled numbers for your final score.

I would like us to be more of a WE rather than two MEs in the following areas of our relationship.

Benefits of Being More of a WE

1. We'd have very good communication. ____

2. We'd have a satisfying sex life. ____

3. We'd organize our home together. ____

4. We'd work toward our goals together ____

5. We'd both help out with household chores as a team. ____

6. We'd both be involved in parenting and being involved with our children. ____

7. We'd be a team in having good relationships with our families. ____

8. We'd have similar beliefs about our basic values in life. ____

9. We'd have similar ideas about how to have a good time and enjoy life. ____

10. We'd be very good friends. ____

11. My partner would give me no reason for feeling jealous. ____

12. We'd be very good at helping each other to reduce stress. ____

13. We'd both feel respected in this relationship. ____

14. We'd both feel loved in this relationship. ____

15. We'd admire one another. ____

16. We'd be confident we could handle any problem we'd face together. ____

17. We'd both feel secure in this relationship. ____

18. We'd get along well with our in-laws. ____

19. We'd share similar views about basic religious or philosophical issues. ____

20. We'd agree on issues related to children. ____

21. We'd have similar views about money. ____

22. We'd know and understand each other. ____

23. We'd both like where we're going in the future. ____

24. We'd both feel that our lives together had purpose and meaning. ____

Add up all your scores for the numbers you circled. If you scored more than 40 points, then this next exercise may be helpful to you.

AREAS FOR BUILDING
WE-NESS (Fill out together)

INSTRUCTIONS. Talk over your individual forms. Then, together, choose one area of your relationship in which to start becoming more of a WE. Try not to struggle over this. Any area where there's improvement means you're becoming more of a WE. Then discuss some alternatives for how that might happen. Write down your ideas in the space below, and commit to following through with one idea in the coming week.

OUR IDEAS:

THIS WEEK, WE COMMIT TO DOING THE FOLLOWING:

THE SECOND STRAND:
BUILDING A HISTORICAL LEGACY

When we become parents, our values, roles, goals, and philosophies of living all transform, too. We're not just daughters and sons. We're mothers and fathers. As we're holding our babies, we gaze in the mirror and in our minds we see photos of our folks holding us. Our childhoods loom large and yet fade around the edges. We see that the legacies we've been left with are ours to transmit, or to discard. Now, as a family, we're newly woven into the web of generations. Who will our children become? And what will they, in turn, pass down?

We're usually ecstatic when our babies are born. We want to carve every moment into memory. So we take photos, save cards, record gurgles, and jot down notes. We frame the first smile, the first giggle, the first crawl, and the first step. We open our childhood albums, and we sing our grandma's lullabies. We cherish our hours together, and we marvel at the speed of their passing. Then we dive deeper.

We remember the old wounds. And we forgive our parents for them. We remember their growls or their silences. But we're dazed by our own sleepless nights. We hear again their sharp words, but we hear their echoes in ourselves. We remember their reins on our pricey desires, but we ponder our own meager accounts. So we worry, we struggle, we fight, and we collapse together in exhaustion. Our compassion toward our parents grows as our consciousness of our own plight awakens. We ask ourselves, how in the world did they do it? And their parents, and the parents before them? Can we learn from them? And should we?

We're creating something brand-new: a family that is a potpourri of cultures. Every family blends together cultural ancestry from both sides. So our relationships are cross-cultural, always. Culture is how we give the ordinary extraordinary meaning. We have many things to decide.

Our vernacular, our styles of dressing, our rituals, our holiday cycles, and our traditions all take on new meaning. Will we light the menorah, or the Christmas lights? Will we celebrate Ramadan? Will we care about image or shun it as bourgeois? Will we give our sons the guns and trucks, or the books about the stars? Will we give our daughters the dress-up dolls, or the white coats and doctors' kits? Which friends will we draw in close, and which ones will we push away? Which family members will we include at dinner, and which ones will we see begrudgingly? Whose cultural values will we embrace? Yours, mine, both, or none?

We pick and choose which ancestors to honor: the noble heroes, the cunning outlaws, or the plain and simple.

In our home in Seattle, we have a wall of pictures. There sit John's parents at their wedding, little John on his rocking horse, baby Julie in her crinoline dress, John's grandfather with his huge butcher's hands, and Julie's father with his spats. There sternly sit Julie's Russian great-grandparents with their seven sons and daughter. And

Julie's father mitted and ready to box. And there we are, jacketed and gowned and newly married. And our daughter gleefully bright at six months. Our crowning glory.

When our daughter was three, we began telling her stories. She heard of brave, caring, and generous people. Like her paternal great-grandfather, the Jewish kosher butcher in Austria. Weekly, he gave a tenth of his meat away to those who were hungry, Jewish or not, and to the Gypsies outside of town. His Sabbath table brimmed over with those he knew, as well as strangers who were just traveling through. There was no fear of those who were different. We told our daughter that we honor his legacy—we also open our door to the community.

Later, we told our daughter about Julie's grandfather, who, at sixteen, walked for two years across Russia to Germany and was chased by sword-wielding Cossacks on horseback. His alternative? To either be killed in village attacks or be conscripted into the army for cannon fodder. And later still, we told her of the twenty-six in John's family who perished in the ovens of Auschwitz and Dachau. And introduced her to the one Dachau-surviving cousin who didn't. We honored John's parents, who ran from Vienna to Switzerland to the Dominican Republic, and Julie's parents, who moved from Detroit to Portland in search of serenity. We told our daughter that she was a Jew.

We showed her the shawl Julie's grandma smuggled out of Russia, the one embroidered in rose and yellow silk blossoms. The one that gleamed on Julie's shoulders in our wedding portrait on the wall. It was our daughter's to wear at her wedding, too, someday, if she wanted to. If she chose to wed, of course.

These were her ancestors, and the beginnings of her legacy.

What is yours?

CREATING A LEGACY: CREATE YOUR OWN WALL OF ANCESTORS

INSTRUCTIONS. Go through your own photo albums of family and friends, and frame the pictures you like best. Include people you admire in your two cultures and histories, even if they are people you don't know. You might also ask your parents to let you copy their photos of old friends and ancestors. Gather the stories of these people, too. Then designate a special place in your home for them—an ancestral corner where your legacy begins.

THE THIRD STRAND: GIVE MEANING TO EVERYDAY EVENTS

In our day-to-day lives, the way we move through time together—when we pause, when we don't; what we see as special and what we deride as banal—reveal our values to our children.

After we had our daughter, we thought about dinner. And not just what to eat. We knew that two-thirds of American families didn't eat together regularly. Of the ones who did, half of the families watched TV during dinner. So first we decided to have our evening meals together, sans TV. It would be a time free of conflict, when we'd share the highlights and lowlights of our day. Then it felt so good to have no TV that we unplugged the box for good. We wanted to be a family who conversed.

Later on, when our daughter was three, John's mother, Lina, complained to us that our daughter didn't kiss her hello and wasn't sad to see her go. We suggested that maybe it was because Lina never visited her much. We'd go out to dinner, but that was too restricted. We told her we wanted her over for our Sabbath meal, but she objected. She was too busy with her friends, and didn't want to be scheduled. However, we insisted, and she finally agreed.

After the first few times, she and our daughter were inseparable. It worked. There was a perfect balance to the four of us sitting at table, praying, singing, and feasting—the three generations together. Then there was one special time when our daughter buried Lina in pillows. They laughed and laughed, and we got it all on film. Now the two of them were all kisses and hugs, spaghetti and ice cream, and it lasted every week for the next seven years.

When Grandma finally came to live with us, our daughter spent hours stroking her and combing her hair. When Lina passed, she left behind a grandchild totally in love with her, who now had her own understanding of "family."

How do we parents blend together a culture of shared meaning that creates a legacy for our children? Whether we realize it or not, we stitch one together with every word, every choice, every silence, and every act. These express our values, our goals, what we deem trivial, and what we find purposeful. What will we do with our twenty-four hours a day?

The ways in which we touch one another emotionally, physically, and spiritually determine who we are as a family. When we practice these moments intentionally, these become our rituals of connection.

Even the small rituals can mean a great deal. Peter and Jill felt very differently about how they'd celebrated Jill's birthday. He said it was fine. She said it was awful. They'd eaten at a romantic restaurant alone, without Baby Anna, and Jill had gotten a present she liked. So what was wrong with that? he wanted to know. Jill replied, "But I made the dinner reservations, and I bought my own present!"

"Right. And I'm a busy physician, and you stay at home. So would it be any different if I had asked my nurse to handle it all? Besides, you never like the presents I pick."

So we asked them to talk about birthdays. As an only child, Jill had had a party every year, with a clown performing magic, and all her friends there. She was totally surprised by all of her presents, and it was the one time a year when she felt loved by her parents. On that day, her parents seemed happy together, too.

Peter, on the other hand, came from a huge family. Like his sibs, he got a birthday card, a present, and one special meal. That was it, said Peter, and that was fine.

"Well, that is not fine with me," said Jill.

But once we started talking about the legacy they were fostering for Anna, their whole focus shifted. Peter admitted that the small presents he got were not always fine. Sometimes one brother got a bigger present than he did. But he convinced himself it was OK, and adjusting to it would just make him stronger. And Jill said that all those presents weren't really what she wanted. She had wanted her parents to be happy with her and happy with each other. But they weren't.

Both Peter and Jill wanted Anna to feel special, but their emotional warmth and their child seeing her parents happy would be the best of all. After talking it through, Peter and Jill designed a birthday ritual that they all could treasure as a family together.

Rituals of connection don't only have to focus on being together "in health." The rest of the wedding vow talks about "in sickness," and we can have rituals for that as well.

One family we knew had to work out major clashes in sick care. Larry's mom had been a busy political activist. She was strong and dynamic, but guilty as all get-out for neglecting her family. So when Larry got sick, she saw her chance at redemption. She'd fluff up his pillows, take his temperature every ten minutes, and shower him with magazines and books. Best of all, she'd make him his favorite lemonade with her own hand-crushed ice. He just loved all that attention.

Now, later in life, Larry married Rita, another strong and dynamic woman. But Rita's experience with illness was an entirely different story. Rita's mother was sick throughout her childhood. She slept in the living room, and family life revolved around her illness. Everyone had to be quiet at all times. But despite all that care, Rita's mom still died of her cancer anyway. At the time, Rita was ten.

Rita and her dad were left behind. They coped with their loss by banding together, toughening up, and getting efficient. If either of them felt in the slightest bit sick, they denied it. Even when she had fevers, Rita went to school, hiding her symptoms from others. Resting when sick was a weakness. Being sick didn't mean being indulged.

One weekend after Larry and Rita had married, Larry, ordinarily a hardy, athletic guy, came down with the flu. He lay in bed all day, feeling miserable. Finally, he cried out in a sulky, whiny voice, "Ri-ieeta." When she ignored him, he again called out, "Riiitaaa." In the laundry room nearby, Rita just rolled her eyes. When she ignored him again, he finally yelled out with desperation, "Riiiiii-eee-ttt-aaaaaahh!!!"

Rita entered his room, wanting to know what catastrophe had happened. Larry pitifully said, "Rita, sweetie, I feel miserable. Can you please fluff up my pillows, get me something to read, and make me some lemonade with hand-crushed ice?"

Rita says that Larry is lucky she didn't murder him. There had been a huge "culture clash." She absolutely couldn't understand what Larry needed. When she felt sick, she was like their cat, who would retreat under the bed and hiss if you tried to pet her. But Larry said no, sickness is a time for love and caring; what about their wedding vows?

Larry and Rita had to work out a ritual around sick care that they both could accept. Rita disclosed how being sick scared the heck out of her, because it was all about her mom dying and leaving her despite the good care and attention she'd received. Rita was also mad that her mom soaked up all the attention with her sickness, though it was tough for her to admit it. Larry shared his resentment that he had had to be sick to get his mom's love and attention at all. Sheepishly, he confessed that every now and then he exaggerated his symptoms just so he could stay home and be pampered. Once the truth was out, Larry and Rita could freely fashion a new ritual around sick care, one that would appropriately nurture both of them as well as their new baby.

We can create rituals of connection around ordinary events and significant ones. What should happen when one of us accomplishes something important? What should happen when one of us fails and needs support? How should we express pride in each other, and in our kids?

Let's start off by exploring how you are currently doing on your rituals of connection.

SELF-TEST ON SHARED RITUALS

Have you and your partner been able to create rituals of emotional connection together that you both value? Check the appropriate TRUE or FALSE box for each item that fits your relationship.

YOUR RITUALS	YOU		YOUR PARTNER	
	T	F	T	F
Reunions at the end of the day in our home are generally special for us.	☐	☐	☐	☐
During weekends, we do a lot of things together that we enjoy and value.	☐	☐	☐	☐
I really look forward to and enjoy our vacations together.	☐	☐	☐	☐
When we do errands together, we generally have a good time.	☐	☐	☐	☐
We have ways of becoming renewed and refreshed when we are burned out or fatigued.	☐	☐	☐	☐

Add up the number of items you checked "True." If you marked fewer than two items, you need to improve in this area of your life together. Read on.

CREATE EVERYDAY RITUALS
OF EMOTIONAL CONNECTION

INSTRUCTIONS. Pick one of the following topics and discuss it with one another. At another time, you can choose one of the other topics to discuss if you like.

1. Talk to each other about family dinnertime in your home. What does eating together mean to you? What are family meals like now? What are some examples of good events and nightmare events around mealtimes when you were each kids? What were these events like for each of you? What did they mean to you, if anything? What is the role of food in your family now?

2. Talk to each other about leave-taking and reunion at the end of the day in your home. What is the reunion like? What goes on? What was it like in your two families growing up? What is important when you all get together at the end of the day? What would you like it to mean?

3. Talk to each other about bedtime in your home. What was it like in your two families growing up? How would you like it to be now? What should it mean?

4. Talk to each other about the weekends. What goes on during the weekends? What were weekends like in your two families growing up? What are some examples of good and bad ones when you were kids? How would you like weekends to be now? What should they mean?

5. Talk to each other about the rituals you have around finances. How do you view money? Why? How was money handled in your two families growing up? What are some examples of good events and nightmare events around money when you were kids? How do you think money should be handled now?

6. Talk to each other about entertaining in your home, having friends over, having parties, and so on. What typically goes on? What was it like in your two families growing up? What are some examples of good events and nightmare events around entertaining when you were kids? What is important to you about entertaining? What atmosphere are you trying to create? What should it mean?

7. What are especially good times for you as a couple, and for your family together? Talk about some recent examples. What was important to you about these times? What were family times like growing up? What kind of good family times do you want to create in your family today?

8. What are typical everyday things you celebrate? Birthdays? Anniversaries? Family reunions? How do you celebrate them? Talk to each other about what these events were like in your two families growing up. What are some examples of good events and nightmare events when you were kids? What do you want these events to mean?

9. What are typical things that happen around someone in your family getting sick? What was being sick like in your family growing up? What do you want it to be like in your own family?

10. Talk about vacations, rituals of renewal of spirit, and travel in your life. What are these events like now for you and what do they mean? What were vacations like in your family growing up? What are some examples of good events and nightmare events when you were kids? What do you want these to be like in your family?

11. Explore recreation rituals that may involve experiences such as dates and getaways, weekend activities, sports events, movies and TV viewing, playtime with the kids, and others. What were these rituals like in your family growing up? What do you want them to be like in your own family?

12. How does your family run errands? What were errands like in your family growing up? What do you want them to be like in your family now?

13. How do you get renewed and refreshed when you are burned out or fatigued? How did your two childhood families do this? How do you want to renew yourselves in your family today?

14. How do you obtain stimulation and enrichment (e.g., through music, plays, art, hobbies, other common interests)? What was enriching in your family growing up? How do you want to enrich yourselves as a family now?

THE FOURTH STRAND: CREATING A SPECIAL HOLIDAY CYCLE

Let's talk about the family holiday cycle. How do you celebrate Thanksgiving, Kwanzaa, Christmas, Passover, or Ramadan . . . and why? Perhaps more than any other event, holidays leave deep tracks in our childhood memory. What imprints do we want our children to have when they're grown up?

Joshua and Tanaya's memories of Christmas were as different as land and sea. For Tanaya, Christmas was a pool of tears. She'd been an only child. Her dad left just before Christmas to serve in Vietnam. She never saw him again. Just before the following Christmas, they learned that he'd fallen in action in Da Nang. Her mother plummeted then into deep depression. Though she improved with time, she never laughed again. Tanaya could never celebrate Christmas after that without feeling the loss of her father's presence and her mother's soul.

But for Joshua, Christmas was different. He had come from a large family in the South. Christmas was the time for family reunions. They'd all attend church, he'd sing in the choir, and they'd feast on steaming barbecue afterward. On Christmas Day, they'd celebrate around the tree and sing Christmas songs, gospel style, and Uncle Stubs would pound on the piano. Joshua never get fancy presents, but he loved Christmas. It was the best time of the year, and he now declared himself a "Christmas junkie." Come June every year, he would secrete away small presents for Tanaya and the kids.

Joshua and Tanaya had to work out a new ritual for Christmas that worked for them both and would yield cherished memories for the kids. They built a special shrine for Tanaya's dad, and lovingly set his picture on it. On the day before Christmas, they honored his memory by telling the kids stories about their grandpa that they would never tire of hearing. Then, on the big day, they freely celebrated Christmas with joy, just the way Joshua had in childhood. When they invited the whole family over so their small home spilled over with children, that was the best part of all.

We get so much more from our holiday rituals when we intentionally create them. Otherwise, if we avoid thinking of them, we "vote with our feet," and our holidays just come up empty. Either way, we are creating the legacy our children will remember.

So many of us want to be as good or better partners and parents than our own parents were. Here's one way to do it: Try creating rituals of connection for your own holiday cycle.

GIVE MEANING TO YOUR OWN YEARLY HOLIDAY CYCLE

INSTRUCTIONS. Together with your partner, pick one holiday from the following list that you want to discuss. Then answer the questions about the holiday you've picked. Later, you can do this again for another in your family's holiday cycle.

Holiday

- Thanksgiving
- Ramadan
- Kwanzaa
- Christmas
- Hanukkah
- Winter solstice
- New Year's
- Any holiday that celebrates the end of winter or the arrival of spring
- Passover
- Easter
- Summer solstice
- Other special holidays for you:

   a.

   b.

   c.

Questions to Answer

- Who do we want to include?
- How do they get invited?
- Who designs and sends the invitations?

- Where should the celebration be held?

- Do we take pictures or videos? Who does the photography?

- What food do we eat? Why those foods in particular?

- Who does what and when? (For example, who shops, and for what kinds of presents? Who cooks, and what are the recipes?)

- What rituals should we do? (For example, at Thanksgiving, we can go around the table and each say what we're thankful for, or at the New Year, share the highlights and lowlights of our last year, plus our resolutions for next year.) What do we want these rituals to mean?

- What's most important about this holiday?

- What is the history of this holiday in our childhood families?

- What stories should be told at these holiday gatherings?

THE FIFTH STRAND: DISCUSS
WHAT OUR ROLES ARE IN OUR LIVES NOW

We all play many roles in life. We are sons or daughters, lovers or friends, workers or players, mothers or fathers. We are sisters or brothers, helpers or builders, followers or leaders. We work, we make money, and we spend money. We are artists, we are mechanics, we are thinkers, and we are scientists. We are athletes, we are sailors, we are protesters, and we are soldiers. The list goes on and on. In all these roles, we can decide who we want to be, and what legacy we'll leave behind. Most of us want to make this world a better place, in whatever ways we can. Take the following self-test, and see if you are building a sense of shared meaning by supporting one another in the roles you've chosen for yourselves.

SELF-TEST: DO YOU
SUPPORT ONE ANOTHER'S ROLES?

YOUR ROLES	YOU		YOUR PARTNER	
We share many similar values in our roles as lovers and partners.	T	F	T	F
My partner and I have compatible views about the role of work in life.	T	F	T	F
My partner and I have similar philosophies about balancing work and family life.	T	F	T	F
My partner supports what I see as my basic mission in life.	T	F	T	F
My partner shares my views on the importance of family and kin (sisters, brothers, moms, dads) in our life together.	T	F	T	F

Add up the number of items you marked "True." If it's two or less, you could do some fine-tuning. If more than two, great!

Roberto and Amber had different ideas about the balance between family, love, and work. They were both biochemists who met over popcorn in a small but prominent biotech firm. When Julia was born, Amber cut back, but Roberto dug in even deeper. Following some terrific successes, he was honored with a grand new project: Could he figure out the genetic basis of diabetes? For many long hours, he slaved at his desk, and at home, burned the midnight oil. Rarely did he come to bed at the same time as Amber, and in the dark she hugged her pillow rather than him. And though he prided himself on being a good dad, Roberto barely played with Julia at all.

When we met Roberto and Amber, they were lonely and alienated and rarely glanced at each other. Amber railed that Roberto didn't support her as a mom, and took her entirely for granted. Roberto claimed that Amber was blind to the importance of his work, and work wasn't a switch he could turn off at bedtime.

"Of course, I get your work, Roberto. After all, I'm a scientist, too.

And I am proud of you. But that doesn't mean you get to cop out as a husband and father."

"Look, I'm working for us all, not just for me."

"I wish you'd work a little harder in bed."

"And I wish you'd shut up your mouth."

Roberto and Amber had a long way to go. They needed to both feel appreciated for what they were giving, and not feel put down for what they were neglecting. They longed for the safety of empathy so they could be vulnerable and say what they needed. As we worked to build a doorway between them, Amber saw that Roberto's work was his mission and not an escape route from his family. Roberto heard that Amber missed his laughter and longed for them all to embrace. In defense, he said he came to bed even when he wanted to work. But Amber replied that him on top of the covers and her beneath them was not what she had in mind.

"Don't you get it? I want to lay my head on your naked, furry chest."

"Oh."

They both missed the tender cuddling they'd shared before. Then Roberto could confess his fear that Julia's best years were passing him by. Slowly, they found their way back to each other by weighing and balancing their roles. Contributing scientist, father, dormant researcher, mother, friend, and lover—all needed definition and rededication. They'd be talking about it for years. But at least they'd made a start.

In our families, we can either support one another in the key roles we play, or not. Here's a way to talk about them.

EXERCISE

YOUR BELIEFS ABOUT THE KEY ROLES YOU PLAY AND HOW TO SUPPORT ONE ANOTHER

INSTRUCTIONS. Give yourselves a good chunk of time. Then pick at least one of the following topics and discuss it with one another.

1. Talk about your own personal view of what being a partner, a mother, and a father means to you. How do you think of yourself in these roles? What is most important to you about each one? What are you trying to accomplish in these roles?

2. Talk about the role of your life work/occupation and what it means to you. What are you trying to accomplish? What is your life mission in your work?

3. How do you balance work and family roles (mother, father, son, daughter, brother, or sister) with your role as a partner or a wife or husband? What limits do you set on each of these roles and why?

4. What about other roles you play, such as provider, protector, nurturer, educator, mentor, friend, and religious or philosophical person? Are any of these roles important to you? Why? How do you see yourself pursuing them?

THE SIXTH STRAND: DEFINE YOUR GOALS

There is a story about Alfred Nobel, the founder of the Nobel Prize. Nobel left behind a legacy that stimulated and celebrated outstanding achievements in literature, science, and the making of peace. Alfred Nobel also happened to invent dynamite. That's how he made his colossal fortune. After the day that Alfred's brother passed away, Stockholm's leading newspaper made a terrible mistake. They thought that Alfred was the one who died; it published a damning obituary of the wrong Nobel. They reported that he had caused more deaths in Europe than any other man who'd ever lived. By inventing dynamite, he had made war the destruction of the best men we had.

Very few of us have the experience of reading our own obituary. It changed Alfred Nobel forever. He set up the Nobel Committee, created the Nobel Prize, and gave much of his fortune to rewarding the creative and the courageous for their work. Nowadays, who recalls that the prizes are based on the dollars from dynamite?

What would you do if you had the chance to write your very own obituary? How would you live your life? Would you make any changes, as did Alfred Nobel? What goals do you have for your life? Does your partner share your view of these goals? And how do you support each other's goals? Are you proud of each other's accomplishments toward them? Take the following self-test to see if you share the same goals and are building shared meaning.

SELF-TEST: DO YOU SHARE COMMON GOALS?

YOUR GOALS	YOU		YOUR PARTNER	
If I were to look back on my life in old age, I think I would see that our paths had meshed.	T	F	T	F
My partner values my accomplishments.	T	F	T	F
My partner honors my personal goals that are unrelated to our relationship.	T	F	T	F
We have very similar financial goals.	T	F	T	F
Our hopes and aspirations, as individuals and together, for our children, for our life in general, and for our old age are quite compatible.	T	F	T	F

Add up the number of items you marked "True." If you checked fewer than two items, you could use some more dialogue. Read on.

Many of us don't think much about our life goals. "If you don't know where you are going," said Yogi Berra, "chances are you'll wind up somewhere else." And Stephen Covey added, "If you don't know where you're headed, it doesn't help to try to go there faster."

Shared goals can be bedrock for our families; they can give us a purposeful pathway that enriches our lives with meaning. To reflect on your family's goals, try this next exercise.

WHAT ARE YOUR COMMON GOALS?

INSTRUCTIONS. Pick at least one of the following topics, and discuss it with one another.

1. If you were able to look back on your life in old age, what would you like to be able to say about your life? What accomplishments would please you?

2. What are some of your personal goals, unrelated to your relationship?

3. What are your financial goals? What financial-disaster scenarios do you want to avoid?

4. What are your hopes and aspirations for your children?

5. What are your life dreams? Why these, and where do you think they come from in your life?

6. Were the goals of your parents similar or different?

7. What goals do you share? What are the discrepancies between your goals? How satisfied are you with this part of your life together? To what extent do you feel that you are actually accomplishing the goals that are important to you?

THE FINAL STRAND: SHARED VALUES AND BELIEFS

Studies reveal that couples who are religious and regularly attend services are no better off than those who don't. Religiosity isn't what matters. Instead, it's whether we view our relationship as sacred, as a covenant never to be broken.

For those of us who consider it sacred, we may believe a higher power has ordained that we be together, or that ethically that's what our commitment means. With either, the findings are that when we consider our relationship sacred, we deal with our conflicts differently. We are more respectful toward one another, and less hostile. We don't escalate into knock-down-drag-outs as often.

Perhaps we are more willing to be a WE rather than a ME, and we more readily accept responsibility for our part in the fight.

How are you doing in sharing your values with each other?

SELF-TEST ON SHARED VALUES

Mark each item TRUE or FALSE.

YOUR VALUES	YOU		YOUR PARTNER	
We see eye-to-eye about what "home" means.	T	F	T	F
We have similar views about the role of sex in our lives.	T	F	T	F
We have similar views about the role of love and affection in our lives.	T	F	T	F
We have similar values about the importance and meaning of money in our lives.	T	F	T	F
We have similar values about "autonomy" and "independence."	T	F	T	F

Add up the number of items you marked "True." If you checked fewer than two items, you could use some more discussion about your values. Read on.

Ethelia and Raymond had a special story to tell. They'd first met on a church committee. Ethelia said that Raymond was the most annoying man she'd ever met. A Baptist minister from rural Louisiana, Raymond described himself as an "earthy" southern man, a man of the land. Ethelia, however, was a woman from the Northwest, raised to consider herself "regal." Men around her, she said, were always polite and respectful. But not Raymond.

The work of the church committee ended, and Ethelia was relieved. But to her own chagrin, she started to miss him. Then one day the phone rang, and it was him!

Raymond and Ethelia went out on their first date in Pike Place Market in Seattle, right after Labor Day. They talked for hours; they lost track of the time. Though surrounded by sweet smells, they even forgot to eat. That evening, Raymond walked her back home. At her door, Raymond took hold of her hand and wouldn't let it go. He whispered, "You know, Ethelia, we are going to be married." She gazed up at him and cried out, "Are you the one?" "Yes, I am," he calmly replied. She then cried buckets and buckets of tears. She knew that he was right.

But there were so many things to work out. Once, in church, she got a splinter in her foot. Raymond immediately hauled out the first-aid kit. Right there, in front of everyone, he kneeled down, took off her shoe, and dug out the splinter. She felt like a farm animal or something, but she couldn't deny his caring. Yet she also had to introduce Raymond to candlelight dinners and the elegance that was her domain. They had to merge their two cultures. Raymond once said, "You can take the man out of the South, but you can't take the South out of the man." Ethelia agreed.

Six weeks after their first date, Raymond, who was a heart patient, had to report for an angiogram. Ethelia showed up at his bedside—with a marriage license and a minister. They married in the cardiac-care unit that day. If anything happened to him, she wanted to be there to care for him. First date after Labor Day, married at Halloween. She was terrified; so was he.

Years later, they told us that when they were about to have an argument, they first separated for a half hour to pray. What did they pray about? we asked. That their partner not be so stubborn? No, they replied, they prayed that they could see their own responsibility for the problem. Once they saw that, and not before, did they come together to discuss their issue. Wow, we thought. That was truly admirable. Their belief that their relationship was sanctified by God had led them to discard defensiveness in their discussions of disagreements.

Raymond and Ethelia rendered their marriage sacred through their shared religious beliefs. But we don't have to be religious to honor our relationships as sacred. Sharing a set of common values and beliefs will do it. The following exercise may help you in identifying your own shared values and beliefs that elevate it to the sacred.

EXERCISE

WHAT ARE YOUR VALUES AND BELIEFS?

INSTRUCTIONS. Pick at least one of the following topics and discuss it with one another.

1. In what ways is your relationship "sacred" to you?

2. What does a "home" mean to you? What does it take to turn a house into a home? What are you doing to create your home together?

3. What does "love" mean to you? How can you manifest it more in your lives?

4. What does being a provider mean to you?

5. What does "spirituality" mean to you? How should it be manifested in your lives?

6. What is the meaning of "peacefulness"? How can you manifest it more in your lives?

7. What is the meaning of "family"? How can you manifest it more in your lives?

8. What does money mean to you? What did money mean to your families growing up? What did you like about that, and what did you dislike? How important should money be in your lives today?

9. What does education mean to you? What did education mean to your families growing up? What did you like about that, and what did you dislike? What are your values about education today? How do you want to manifest them?

10. What do "fun" and "play" mean to you? What role should they play in your life together?

11. What is the meaning to you of "trust"?

12. What is the meaning to you of "freedom," of "autonomy," of "independence," and of "power"?

13. What is the meaning to each of you of being "interdependent," of being a "WE"?

14. What is the meaning of "having possessions," of "owning things" (like cars, nice clothes, books, music, a house, and land)?

15. What is the meaning of "nature" to you? What is your relationship to the seasons?

16. What do you reminisce about?

SUMMARY

In this chapter, we've looked at how we can create legacies for our children, and how we can deepen our lives together with meaning. We've talked of ancestry, of everyday moments, and of holidays. We've reviewed our roles, our goals, and our values. Our journeys through time together can be graced with discussions like these. And because we are constantly changing, these discussions will never end. Like the loaf and fish that multiplied, they can feed us for a lifetime.

So mix the ingredients: Savor the friendship, delight in your children, cool down your conflicts, add in warm fathering, savor your sex life, and now braid together what gives your lives meaning. Bake it in the warmth of your home. Now you've got good bread.

ACKNOWLEDGMENTS

This project has been fifteen years in the making. There are so many people to thank. What follows is by no means a complete list, which would take a chapter by itself to complete. But we'll start at the beginning. Fourteen years ago, John built the apartment lab. The lab looked like a bed-and-breakfast room, with a few small exceptions. There were three cameras bolted to the walls, a one-way window, a separate conflict discussion room, and a control room that monitored the video and synchronized with the couples' physiology. We studied 130 newlywed couples for six years after their weddings. They were filmed, their autonomic physiology was measured, their urine was collected and tested for stress hormones, and their blood was sent to Dr. Hans Ochs's lab to study immune system properties. Our phenomenal team gathered the data. Thanks to Dr. Sybil Carrere, Jim Coan, Jani Driver, Sonny Ruckstahl, Kim McCoy, and a host of undergraduate volunteers, this study yielded important knowledge on the nature of relationships.

As the first fifty couples in this study became parents, they were again observed together with their babies, using the methods of the brilliant Dr. Elizabeth Fivaz-Depeursinge and Antoinette Corbez-Warnery. Thanks to them for their consultation with us.

Later Alyson Shapiro joined our staff, quickly distinguished herself as a natural leader, and gathered together a team of undergraduate volunteers. John had won the James Mifflin Chair at the University of Washington, and with those monies, funded by the Huckabee family, he designed interventions to prevent the decay of parents' relationships after their baby's arrival. With Alyson and the team, especially Brandi Fink and Cindy Davis, the first randomized clinical trials were run.

Swedish Medical Center staff members Katie Broch, Debbie Sibolski, and Jodi Olson offered to host the BBH research project in the Center's childbirth education department. Working countless hours, three childbirth educators, Carolyn Pirak, Joni Parthemer, and Rosalys Peel, helped John and Julie to develop the Bringing Baby Home workshop. They continue to work with us today. Carolyn Pirak, our BBH workshop national director, has trained and certified hundreds of other BBH workshop leaders in twenty-four countries around the world. Her tireless dedication and that of her team is beyond measure.

Five years ago, Ron Rabin walked into John's office. He is the executive director of the Kirlin Foundation, formed by Dan and Sally Kranzler. Ron asked John if he needed any money for research. John was dumbfounded. Does a man in the desert need water? He just nodded yes. Later, Craig Stewart, director of the Apex Foundation, expressed the desire to help us as well. From there, Bruce and Jolene McCaw, donors of the Apex Foundation and founders of the Talaris Research Institute, joined with Dan and Sally Kranzler to generously fund the second Bringing Baby Home research study. We owe great thanks to them and to the Talaris Research Institute staff as well: Buck Smith, Terry Meersman, Bridgett Chandler, and Alden Jones. This work would have been impossible without their open-hearted belief in us.

Alyson Shapiro, and, later, Dan Yoshimoto, ran the Bringing Baby Home research project with tremendous attention to detail and wonderful morale. Our sterling staff included: Chrissy Anderson, Erin Allen Brower, Kristi Content, Elizabeth Coleman, Cindy Davis, Jani Driver, Kaeleen Drummey, Brandi Fink, Kelly Green,

Acknowledgments

Kristin Johnson, Julia Laibson, Betty Lopez, Nicki Fischer Meyers, Dr. James Murray, Eun Young Nahm, Elizabeth Schoettle, Katherine Schwartz, Catherine Swanson, Marina Smith, Amber Tabares, Lisa Taylor, and Becky Thatcher. They were simply the best at every aspect of this work. Special thanks also go to our Jill-of-all-Trades, Sharon Fentiman, John's devoted administrative assistant for many years at the University of Washington, and our dear friend Derk Jager; together, they formed our project videography team.

Finally, our deepest thanks to our brilliant agent, Katinka Matson, who was instrumental in developing the proposal for this book. Without her belief in us, there would be no book. And thanks to the superb staff at Crown, especially Kristin Kiser and Tara Gilbride, who have guided this book to publication.

INDEX

Index

criticism, 17, 24, 57–58, 130
crying, 9, 19, 37, 40, 45, 215
cuddling, 37, 53, 189
culture, 27, 219

dating, 18
Davidson, Richard, 43
deep muscle relaxation, 87
Defending the Caveman (play), 185
defensiveness, 17, 109
   conflict and, 24, 130
   harsh start-ups and, 57, 58
   summarizing yourself syndrome
     and, 67, 80
De Lee, Joseph, 194
depression
   in babies, 28, 43
   brain activity and, 43
   massage benefits for, 169
   parental exhaustion and, 8, 20
   postpartum, 8, 11, 36, 201
   in quarantined children, 40
desire. *See* sexual desire
development, 9–10, 11, 28–29
   emotional, 9, 11, 28, 189–90, 201
   enhancement of, 11, 189–90, 201
   intellectual, 9, 190, 201
   time scale for, 33–34
Diallo, Amadou, 79
dialogue, 54, 129–44
Dick-Read, Grantly, 198
diffuse physiological arousal (DPA),
   77–87
disaster couples, 5, 6, 8–10, 67, 99
disrespect, 17, 24, 58
distance, emotional, 176
division of labor, 8, 20–22, 184–85
divorce, 18, 58
domestic violence, 18, 109
"do-touch" nursery schools, 169
doulas, 36, 193
DPA. *See* diffuse physiological
   arousal (DPA)
dreams, 6, 136, 137–40
"dreams-within-conflict" method, 54,
   138–44
Driver, Janice, 99

egalitarian partnership, 190–91
   division of labor and, 8, 20–22,
     184–85

Ekman, Paul, 59
emotional availability, 23, 40, 48
emotional connection
   between parent and child, 9, 28–29,
     39
   between parents/partners, 6, 9–10,
     153
emotional development, 9, 11, 28,
   189–90, 201
emotional distance, 176
emotional intimacy, 8, 23, 26
emotion coaching, 189
emotions
   brain activity and, 42–43
   positive and negative, 11
empathy, 189
evolution, 78
exercises and self-tests
   acceptance of influence, 71
   ancestors' wall, 221
   appreciation expression, 150–52
   beliefs about men, 186–87
   common goals, 234, 235
   compromise, 96–98
   dreams within conflict, 140–44
   effective repair, 100–103
   emotional withdrawal and
     loneliness, 82–83
   fight-aftermath processing, 109–13,
     121–23
   flooding, 81, 87–88
   Four Horsemen, 131
   gridlock, 131–32
   holiday cycle meaning, 229–30
   ME to WE, 216–17
   needed conversations, 180–81
   open-ended questions, 148–49
   perpetual issues, 127–29, 131–32
   Rapoport Method, 71–73
   relationship with own father,
     187–88
   rituals of connection, 226–27
   role support, 231, 232–33
   self-soothing, 88–91
   sex life evaluation, 162–64
   shared rituals, 225
   shared values, 236
   softened start-ups, 62–63
   start-ups, 61–62
   turning toward partner's needs,
     154–55

ABOUT THE AUTHORS

JOHN M. GOTTMAN, Ph.D., and JULIE SCHWARTZ GOTTMAN, Ph.D., are the authors of *Ten Lessons to Transform Your Marriage* and the founders and the directors of the Gottman Institute and the Relationship Research Institute in Seattle. The bestselling author of *The Seven Principles for Making Marriage Work* and *The Relationship Cure*, among other books, John Gottman is an emeritus professor of psychology, an elected fellow of the American Psychological Association, executive director of the Relationship Research Institute, and the recipient of numerous awards and commendations. His research and findings have been featured in the *Wall Street Journal*, *Time*, the bestselling book *Blink*, and in the broadcast media. Julie Schwartz Gottman established the Gottman Institute's Marriage Clinic and serves as its clinical director. She is also the founder and clinical director of "Loving Couples Loving Children," a curriculum for couples coping with extraordinary stresses. A clinical psychologist, she is in private practice in Seattle, where the couple lives.